Public Record Office Handbooks
No. 24

English Sheriffs to 1154

Judith A. Green

HMSO: LONDON

© *Crown copyright 1990*
First published 1990

ISBN 0 11 440236 1

British Library Cataloguing in Publication Data.

*A CIP catalogue of this book
is available from the British Library.*

Contents

Preface

The lists have been a lengthy production, and the author would like to thank all librarians for access to manuscripts consulted in the search for sheriffs, especially those of Balliol College Oxford, the Bodleian Library, the British Library, Cambridge University Library, Christ's College Cambridge, Durham Dean and Chapter, Hertfordshire County Record Office, the Huntington Library at San Marino, John Rylands Library, Kent Record Office, Lambeth Palace, Lincoln's Inn, the Public Record Office at Chancery Lane, Westminster Abbey, and York Dean and Chapter. Special thanks must be given to Professor H.S. Offler for help with and references to early sheriffs of Durham, and to Dr P. McNiven of the John Rylands Library for allowing me to see *The Charters of the Anglo–Norman Earls of Chester c. 1071–1237* in advance of publication, thus making it possible to include a list of the sheriffs of Cheshire. Those who have over the years discussed sheriffs and the problems of listing them include Professor C.N.L. Brooke who learnt of the project at an early stage, supplied the author with his own unpublished lists, and has since encouraged publication; Mr Patrick Wormald who commented on the early sheriffs and Dr David Bates who commented on the sheriffs mentioned in the *regesta* of William the Conqueror, and has supplied copies of texts in advance of publication in his new edition of the *regesta*; also Miss C. Clark, Dr D. Crouch, Miss E. Danbury, Dr I. Green, Dr D.E. Greenway, Dr E. van Houts, Mr C.J. McNamee, Dr J. Palmer, Dr A. Rumble, and Dr A. Williams. Finally, thanks are due to Queen's University, Belfast, for financial support for research trips over a period of years, to its librarians for their help in obtaining rare books, and to Dr M.R. Foster of the Public Record Office for guiding the manuscript towards publication.

Judith A. Green
Department of Modern History
The Queen's University of Belfast

List of abbreviations

ASC
: *The Anglo-Saxon Chronicle: a revised translation*, ed. D. Whitelock, D.C. Douglas and S.I. Tucker (London, 1961).

ASChs.
: *Anglo-Saxon Charters*, ed. A.J. Robertson (Cambridge, 1939).

B and C
: T.A.M. Bishop, and P. Chaplais, *Facsimiles of English Royal Writs to A.D. 1100 presented to V.H. Galbraith* (Oxford, 1957).

BF
: *Book of Fees: Liber Feodorum. The Book of Fees commonly called Testa de Nevill, reformed from the earliest MSS, by the Deputy Keeper of the Records* (London, 1920–31).

Beauchamp Cart.
: *The Beauchamp Cartulary Charters 1100–1268*, ed. E. Mason (Pipe Roll Society, new series, XLIII, 1980 for 1971–3).

BL
: British Library.

Cart. Aldgate
: *Cartulary of Holy Trinity Aldgate*, ed. G.A.J. Hodgett (London Record Society, VII, 1971).

Cart. Boxgrove
: *The Cartulary of Boxgrove Priory*, ed. L. Fleming (Sussex Record Society, LIX, 1960).

Cart. Colchester
: *Cartularium de Colecestria*, ed. S.A. Moore (2 vols., Roxburghe Club, 1897).

Cart. Colne
: *Cartularium Prioratus de Colne*, ed. E.J. Fisher (Essex Archaeological Society Occasional Publications, I, 1946).

Cart. Eynsham
: *Eynsham Cartulary*, ed. H.E. Salter (2 vols., Oxford Historical Society, XLIX, LI, 1907–08).

Cart. Glouc.
: *Historia et Cartularium Monasterii Sancti Petri Gloucestriae*, ed. W. Hart (3 vols., Rolls Series, London, 1863–7).

Cart. Launceston
: *The Cartulary of Launceston Priory*, ed. P.L. Hull (Devon and Cornwall Record Society, new series, XXX, 1987).

Cart. Lewes
: *The Chartulary of the Priory of St Pancras of Lewes*, ed. L.F. Salzman (2 vols., Sussex Record Society, XXXVIII, XL, 1933–5).

Cart. Missenden
: *The Cartulary of Missenden Abbey*, ed. J.G. Jenkins (2 vols., Buckinghamshire Record Society, II, X, 1939 for 1938, 1955).

Cart. Oseney
: *Cartulary of Oseney Abbey*, ed. H.E. Salter, (6 vols., Oxford Historical Society, LXXXIX–XCI, XCVII–XCVIII, CI, 1929–1936).

Cart. Ram.
: *Cartularium Monasterii de Ramesia*, ed. W.H. Hart and P.A. Lyons (3 vols., Rolls Series, London, 1884–93).

Cart. St Frideswide
: *Cartulary of the Monastery of St Frideswide*, ed. S.R. Wigram (Oxfordshire Historical Society, XXVIII, XXXI, 1895–6).

Cart. Sele
: *Chartulary of the Priory of St Peter at Sele*, ed. L.F. Salzman (Cambridge, 1923).

Cart. Shrewsbury
: *The Cartulary of Shrewsbury Abbey*, ed. U. Rees (2 vols., Aberystwyth, 1975).

Cart. Worc.
: *The Cartulary of Worcester Cathedral Priory*, ed. R.R. Darlington (Pipe Roll Society, LXXVI, 1968 for 1962–3).

CDF
: *Calendar of Documents preserved in France, illustrative of the History of Great Britain and Ireland*, I, *A.D. 918–1216*, ed. J.H. Round (London, 1899).

Chron. Abingdon
: *Chronicon Monasterii de Abingdon*, ed. J. Stevenson (2 vols., Rolls Series, London, 1858).

Chron. Battle
: *The Chronicle of Battle Abbey*, ed. and trans. E. Searle (Oxford, 1980).

Chron. Melsa
: *Chronica Monasterii de Melsa*, ed. E.A. Bond (3 vols., Rolls Series, London, 1866–8).

Chron. Ram.	*Chronicon Abbatiae Ramesiensis*, ed. W. Dunn Macray (Rolls Series, London, 1886).
CUL	Cambridge University Library.
DB	*Domesday Book seu Liber Censualis Willelmi Primi Regis Angliae*, I, II, ed. A. Farley, III, IV, ed. H. Ellis (4 vols., Record Commission, London, 1783–1816). References are to this edition unless otherwise stated.
DK Report 31	*Thirty-first Report of the Deputy Keeper of the Public Records* (London, 1870).
DK Report 35	*Thirty-fifth Report of the Deputy Keeper of the Public Records* (London, 1874).
EHR	*English Historical Review.*
EYC	*Early Yorkshire Charters*, I–III, ed. W. Farrer (Edinburgh, 1914–16); IV–XII, ed. C.T. Clay (Yorkshire Archaeological Society, record series, extra series, I–III, V–X, 1935–65).
FDBSE	*Feudal Documents from the Abbey of Bury St Edmunds*, ed. D.C. Douglas (British Academy, Records of the Social and Economic History of England and Wales, London, 1932).
FW	Florence of Worcester, *Chronicon ex Chronicis*, ed. B. Thorpe (2 vols., London, 1848, 1849).
Harmer	Harmer, F.E. *Anglo-Saxon Writs* (Manchester, 1952).
Hatton's Book of Seals	*Sir Christopher Hatton's Book of Seals*, ed. L.C. Loyd and D.M. Stenton (Northamptonshire Record Society, XV, 1950).
HMC 3rd Report	*Third Report of the Royal Commission on Historical Manuscripts* (London, 1872).
HMC 8th Report	*Eighth Report of the Royal Commission on Historical Manuscripts* (London, 1881).
HMC 9th Report	*Ninth Report of the Royal Commission on Historical Manuscripts* (London, 1883).
HMC Wells, I	*Calendar of the Manuscripts of the Dean and Chapter of Wells*, I (Historical Manuscripts Commission, London, 1907).
JW	*The Chronicle of John of Worcester*, ed. J.R.H. Weaver, (Anecdota Oxoniensia, mediaeval and modern series, XII, Oxford, 1908).
LE	*Liber Eliensis*, ed. E.O. Blake, Camden Society, 3rd Series, XCII (1962).
Magnum Registrum Album	*The Great Register of Lichfield Cathedral, known as Magnum Registrum Album*, ed. H.E. Savage (William Salt Archaeological Society, third series, 1926 for 1924).
Mon. Ang.	W. Dugdale, *Monasticon Anglicanum* (new edn, 6 vols. in 8, London, 1817–30).
OV	Orderic Vitalis, *The Ecclesiastical History*, ed. M. Chibnall (6 vols., Oxford, 1969–1980).
PR 31 Henry I	*Magnum Rotuli Scaccarii vel Magnum Rotulum Pipae de Anno Tricesimo-primo Regni Henrici Primi*, ed. J. Hunter (Record Commission, London, 1833).
PR 2–4 Henry II	*The Great Rolls of the Pipe for the Second, Third, and Fourth Years of the Reign of King Henry the Second, 1155–1158*, ed. J. Hunter (Record Commission, London, 1844).
PR 6 Henry II	*The Great Roll of the Pipe for the Sixth Year of the Reign of King Henry the Second* (Pipe Roll Society, II, 1884).
PR 7 Henry II	*The Great Roll of the Pipe for the Seventh Year of the Reign of King Henry the Second* (Pipe Roll Society, IV, 1885).
PRO	Public Record Office, London.
PRO Revised List	*List of Sheriffs for England and Wales from the earliest Times to A.D. 1831 compiled from documents in the Public Record Office. Lists and Indexes* IX, Public Record Office (originally published London, 1898; reprinted with amendments by M. Mills, New York, 1963).
RBE	*Red Book of the Exchequer*, ed. H. Hall (3 vols., Rolls Series, London, 1896).
RRAN	*Regesta Regum Anglo–Normannorum 1066–1154*, I, ed. H.W.C. Davis, II, ed. C. Johnson and H.A. Cronne, III and IV, ed. H.A. Cronne and R.H.C. Davis (4 vols., Oxford, 1913–69).
Reg. Antiq.	*Registrum Antiquissimum of the Cathedral Church of Lincoln*, ed. C.W. Foster and K. Major (10 vols., Lincoln Record Society, 1931–68).

Robertson	Robertson, A.J., *Anglo-Saxon Charters* (2nd edn, Cambridge, 1956).
S	P.H. Sawyer, *Anglo-Saxon Charters: an Annotated List and Bibliography* (Royal Historical Society, London, 1968).
SD	Symeon of Durham, *Opera Omnia*, ed. T. Arnold (2 vols., Rolls Series, London, 1882–5).
St Radegund	A. Gray, *The Priory of St Radegund* (Cambridge, 1898).
Sarum Charters	*Charters and Documents illustrating the History of the Cathedral, City, and Diocese of Salisbury in the Twelfth and Thirteenth Centuries*, selected by W. Rich Jones and ed. W. Dunn Macray (Rolls Series, London, 1891).
VCH	*The Victoria History of the Counties of England* (London, 1900, in progress).
WM	William of Malmesbury, *De Gestis Pontificum Anglorum Libri Quinque*, ed. N.E.S.A. Hamilton (Rolls Series, London, 1870).

Introduction

The Office

The emergence of sheriffs or shire-reeves as distinct from other reeves mentioned in tenth-century sources cannot be pinpointed with any precision. The shiring of England was a lengthy and complex process, not complete by the Norman Conquest.[1] By the early eleventh century the midlands and the south had been shired. Some boundaries, such as those of Kent and Sussex reflected earlier kingdoms, whilst others, notably in the midland counties, took account of more recent developments. The east midland counties, for instance, corresponded to territories dependent on fortified towns, or burhs, and were only taking their final shape in the early eleventh century.[2] North of the Humber and the Mersey older regional units survived: Yorkshire was a vast sprawling region; the area west of the Pennines and north of the Mersey was simply described as 'between Ribble and Mersey', whilst beyond the Ribble the influence of the southern kings faded out; and beyond the Tees in the north-east lay the lands of the bishopric of Durham and remote Northumberland, rump of the old Bernician kingdom.[3] The slow stabilization of county boundaries has to be borne in mind when considering the origins of the shrievalty.

The description shire-reeve does not occur until the earlier years of Cnut's reign, in Kent and Staffordshire.[4] Before that date, there are men described as reeves or high reeves, some of whom may have been in charge of shires.[5] In addition there are two references to 'shire-men' who have stronger claims to be classed as sheriffs: the earliest is to Wulfsige the priest, shire-man of Kent, who is mentioned in a charter dated between 964 and 988; the second, also from Kent, is dated between 995 and 1006.[6] If these men were the earliest identifiable sheriffs, then the office may be dated back at least to Edgar's reign.

W.A. Morris, who wrote a classic study of the medieval shrievalty, believed that the office emerged during Edgar's reign, and was connected with the establishment of the peacekeeping role of hundreds and wapentakes prescribed in King Edgar's Ordinance of the Hundred.[7] That Ordinance laid down the duties of hundred courts meeting every four weeks with particular concern for the pursuit of thieves.[8] Hundreds and, in the north and east, wapentakes, were territorial subdivisions of the shires. Some hundreds were evidently ancient territories paying dues at royal estates;[9] others were newer and cut across estate and settlement distribution.[10] The duties laid down for hundreds in Edgar's Ordinance developed from earlier associations for the maintenance of order; nevertheless it represented an important step in the transfer of duties of justice and police from kindred groups to territorial units.[11] Morris believed that the first sheriffs had taken over the powers previously held by reeves of burghal districts, and had shifted part of the responsibility of the latter onto smaller administrative units, thus explaining the later powers of sheriffs over hundreds and wapentakes. Morris's argument that the rise of the shrievalty was specifically linked with the peacekeeping role of the hundred is not altogether convincing. It was after all the unit smaller than the shire that was envisaged as the key in tackling theft, unless it is argued that groups of hundreds needed supervision by a shire-reeve.

The need for a shire-reeve is more readily explicable in a context broader than that of supervising only the judicial work of the hundreds. The emergence of shires and their reeves is rather a reflection of the growing power of tenth-century monarchy to intervene in the localities, and an increasing need for reeves to coordinate the administration of royal rights and collection of dues at the shire level. The emergence of the shires and shire-reeves could thus be seen as a gradual development, possibly beginning earlier than Edgar's reign. A critical period seems to have been the reign of Aethelred, who was faced with the difficult task of raising men and money to meet the Danish invasions over a protracted period. At the same time he was evidently unable to rely on the loyalty of all of the ealdormen, great magnates who acted as the king's regional representatives with military and political functions. The threat posed by uncertain loyalties could well explain a growing reliance on reeves in charge of smaller units than ealdormanries.[12] At the same time repeated levies of men and money required supervision of local effort. In the eleventh century gelds are known to have been apportioned on the county and the burden subdivided amongst hundreds: reeves at the county level were needed to ensure that the hundredmen did collect the money.[13] Although Cnut was to revive provincial units of government by appointing earls, sheriffs remained as their deputies. The origins of the shrievalty may go back to Edgar's reign if not earlier, but the decisive stimulus may well have been the prolonged difficulties faced by Aethelred.

The growing prominence of shire courts in the eleventh century is reflected in royal writs, surviving in increasing numbers from Aethelred's reign. Writs were usually addressed to locally prominent men: bishops, earls, stallers, sheriffs, and sometimes to individuals addressed simply by name, and it has been suggested that they represented notifications to shire courts of lawsuits or land grants. As such they were much shorter than solemn charters which provided a formal record of transactions.[14] Writs therefore supply additional names of sheriffs from the early eleventh century. Nevertheless many gaps in the evidence remain, and it is only with the retrospective information supplied by Domesday Book that sheriffs may be identified in many counties on the eve of the Norman Conquest.

Before 1066 sheriffs thus occur chiefly as judicial and financial officials. In the shire courts they sat with bishops, ealdormen or earls, and leading thegns. It was in this court meeting usually twice each year that major lawsuits over land were settled: Wulfsige the priest, for instance, was present when Archbishop Dunstan of Canterbury vindicated the claims of the church of St Andrew of Rochester to an estate at Wouldham in Kent before an assembly that included the bishops of London and Rochester, the monastic communities of Christ Church Canterbury and Rochester, and all the men of east and west Kent.

As the great men of church and state had responsibilities which engaged them elsewhere, sheriffs must often have presided in the shire courts, which dealt with a wide range of land actions, both before and after the Norman Conquest; and they also probably dealt with criminal matters before the advent of royal justices in the localities.[15]

It is not clear how actively sheriffs intervened in hundred and wapentake courts before the Conquest. Those courts had important duties in connexion with thief-catching and in general tended to deal with local issues, 'cases between vills and neighbours' as described in a collection of laws made in the twelfth century.[16] Hundreds were also involved in arrangements for suretyship, or 'borh', by which tithings (in most parts of the country groups of ten men) stood surety for each other's good behaviour and appearance in court. Tithings were subdivisions of hundreds, and it was in the hundred court that by the twelfth century if not earlier, sheriffs twice each year checked that the tithings were full, in a procedure called the view of frankpledge.[17]

Hundreds and wapentakes were also used as administrative units for other purposes, notably the assessment of public burdens such as geld and military service. Geld had been collected at least from the time of Aethelred to pay off the Danes and to raise money for troops. The Norman kings found it too useful to abandon. Although it may have been dropped in the last years of Henry I's reign, and possibly during that of his successor, it was briefly revived by Henry II.[18] By the twelfth century pipe rolls reveal the sheriffs' responsibility for the geld collected in their shires by local collectors. By that time sheriffs were the king's chief financial officers in the localities. The management of most royal estates was supervised by the sheriff, who paid over a consolidated sum, the county farm, comprising the rents not only from royal manors but also from boroughs, and certain judicial fines.[19] Quite how far royal land management had been channelled through the hands of the sheriff before the Conquest is not entirely clear.[20] Sheriffs certainly held individual manors at farm, and Domesday Book suggests that the sheriff of one county, Warwickshire, had paid a farm for the county.[21] County farms may not have been established as a general rule before the

i.e.
sheriff

Conquest: in the immediate post-Conquest years the amount of land coming into and out of direct royal control would have made it difficult to keep track of the sums due from sheriffs, and so perhaps it was only as the period of massive redistribution came to an end that county farms were imposed.[22]

Again it is only from the first surviving pipe roll that the sheriffs' responsibilities for transferring other revenues from the shire to the treasury can be documented, although it is likely that they were far from novel in the early twelfth century. At that time sheriffs collected some of the fines imposed in shire and hundred courts, and fines imposed on local communities, such as murder fines, which had been introduced by the Conqueror to protect the lives of his followers.[23]

Although most of the surviving references to early sheriffs relate to their judicial and financial duties, it is possible they had other functions only dimly perceived in the sources. Domesday Book shows, for instance, that sheriffs of the border counties of Shropshire and Herefordshire were able to call out local levies;[24] and in 1056 Aelfnoth, sheriff of Herefordshire, had been killed in battle against the Welsh.[25] Perhaps other sheriffs also had military responsibilities, although it is equally possible to argue that the ealdormen or earls would usually have taken charge.[26] After the Conquest less is heard about the sheriff's duties in connexion with military obligations, either those surviving from the past or the newer obligations to knight service.[27] Some sheriffs were given custody of the castles built in major towns after the Conquest, but there is no evidence that that was a matter of course before 1154.[28]

Before the Conquest little is heard of sheriffs as executive officers of the crown, although this had become a vital aspect of their work by the twelfth century. Before 1066 sheriffs were often addressed in royal writs, but these were usually notifications to the shire court of decisions or appointments already made by the king, not mandates requiring executive action. It has been pointed out that there would have been little reason to preserve executive writs of only short-term importance;[29] on the other hand it may be misleading to assume that already before 1066 the crown was using sheriffs as executive officers as regularly as it was to do in the twelfth century.

From the Conquest, writs survive addressed to the sheriff, ordering him, for instance, to convene shire or hundred courts, to put named individuals in seisin of land, to restore fugitives to their lords, or to execute judgments. Sometimes the sheriff is simply ordered 'to do right' in a particular matter; conversely he might be warned to protect someone from being brought to court.[30]

Before the Norman Conquest sheriffs were not supreme in the localities, where the most powerful representatives of the king in the political and military spheres were first ealdormen and then, from Cnut's reign, earls. Ealdormen and earls were appointed by the king, and usually held more than one county; the boundaries of ealdormanries often reflected earlier political units, whereas earldoms were created and broken up rather more freely.[31] Little can be said of the relationships between ealdormen or earls and sheriffs before the Conquest, other than to point to the lack of evidence suggesting sheriffs were commended to earls.[32] Earls sat with bishops and sheriffs in the shire courts, and apparently took a share of the fines imposed there.[33] Stallers also appear in eleventh-century sources. The word 'staller' means place man, and it was used of men close to the king. In several writs of the Confessor's reign stallers are amongst those addressed, in such a way as to suggest that they may have had local responsibilities.[34] This has led some historians to conclude that stallers sometimes acted as sheriffs. Yet the writs concerned were all issued in favour of Westminster abbey, and the address to stallers (amongst others) may simply reflect a preference for using them to implement grants to an abbey with whose endowment King Edward was so closely concerned, rather than their tenure of shrievalties.[35]

After the battle of Hastings Earls Edwin of Mercia and Morcar of Northumbria survived under the new régime until 1071.[36] No successor was appointed to Edwin as earl of Mercia, but both William the Conqueror and William Rufus continued the practice of appointing earls for Northumbria. Successive earls, however, were defeated either by the instability of the political situation in the north or because they became embroiled in revolts against the crown.[37] The Latin word for earl was *comes*, a title reserved in Normandy for an élite minority. The Norman kings were similarly sparing with the title in England. Adding to the men already of comital status when they arrived in England, William the Conqueror conferred the title on Odo bishop of Bayeux, William FitzOsbern, and two other men who were each given a county on the borders of Wales, Roger of Montgomery (Shropshire) and Hugh d'Avranches (Cheshire).[38] Those counties each had sheriffs, but as long as the Norman earldoms endured (until 1102 and 1237 respectively) the earls controlled the sheriffs.[39] Three or four additional earls were created by William Rufus, namely, Surrey, Warwick, Huntingdon and possibly Buckingham; Henry I added Leicester and Gloucester.[40] Yet these new creations, whose powers were, like those of Roger of Montgomery and Hugh d'Avranches, confined to single counties, did not remove the sheriffs from royal control. The precedence of earls over sheriffs was recognized, for instance, in the address clauses of royal writs,[41] but the crown could still communicate directly with the sheriffs, and in 1130 the sheriffs of all counties with earls, except Cheshire, accounted at the Exchequer.

The fact that only a handful of counties had earls in the Conqueror's day meant that in most counties it was the sheriff who was the local representative of royal authority. That situation began to change as the crown increasingly used local magnates as justices, either specially commissioned or, by the third decade of Henry I's reign at the latest, travelling through the shires hearing royal pleas.[42] It is difficult to be sure how far first local justiciars and then itinerant justices diminished the sheriffs' importance in hearing royal pleas because so little is known about the preceding period, but their very presence in the localities provided a check to the sheriffs' independence.

The development of the Exchequer provided another check, helping to weave the sheriff's office more closely into a web of centralized government. The Exchequer was a court of audit meeting twice each year at Easter and Michaelmas in the treasury, to scrutinize the accounts presented by sheriffs and other financial agents. Its name was taken from the checked cloth on a table round which sat leading members of the royal household. The sums which the sheriff owed and those which he actually paid, together with authorized expenditure and allowances, were set out on the checked cloth, so that all present were fully apprised of the situation, for the sheriff was held accountable for any sums outstanding. The word 'Exchequer' first appears in 1110 and the checked cloth may have been introduced in that year, but there may have been an earlier court of audit, for we are told by the author of the twelfth-century treatise on the operation of the Exchequer that its old name had been 'at the tallies' from the wooden tallies given to sheriffs as receipts.[43] There are indications of such a court in the reign of William Rufus, although some historians would argue that its origins go back before the Conquest.[44] Its primary function was to enforce accountability. Hence the insistence by the author of the *Dialogus de Scaccario* on the accuracy of the record kept, and the obligations of the sheriffs. Appearing before the court must have been a solemn occasion: one sheriff in Henry I's reign, Gilbert the knight, was described as the only sheriff to have been cheerful at meetings of the Exchequer.[45]

The routine described in the *Dialogus* had evidently been established by the time of the first surviving pipe roll. At Easter a preliminary view was taken, and the final account was heard at Michaelmas. The monies brought by the sheriff for the farm were checked for quality at that time and a surcharge imposed if the coins were too obviously lightweight.[46] As well as the county farm the sheriff also accounted for any royal woods in his custody, for judicial payments outside the farm, and for aids or gelds.

This system came under great pressure and broke down during the troubled reign of Stephen. The author of the *Dialogus* relates how on the accession of Henry II the bishop of Ely, Henry I's treasurer, was called in to restore the knowledge of the Exchequer, 'which had almost perished during the long years of civil war'.[47] The author may have exaggerated for reasons of family pride, the bishop of Ely, whose achievement he compares with that of Ezra, the restorer of the scriptures, being his uncle. Nevertheless there is no doubt that there was at least a partial breakdown, as is apparent from the disarray recorded in the financial accounts of the early years of Henry II's reign.[48]

At first Stephen seems to have coped reasonably well, the serious breakdown occurring a few years after the start of the reign. He presumably inherited a full set of sheriffs from his uncle, and there are indications that in a few counties Henrician sheriffs stayed in post.[49] As Stephen ran into difficulties, his response to the problem of keeping control of the localities was greatly to increase the numbers of earls.[50] Earls were appointed to most counties by 1140, and Stephen seems either to have allowed them to take charge of the sheriffs or to have been unable to prevent them from doing so. Documents survive for several earldoms addressed by earls to 'their' sheriffs in particular counties where previously there had been royal sheriffs.[51] Moreover at the first Michaelmas audit after Stephen's death, earls were accounting directly to the Exchequer for Devon, Norfolk, Suffolk, and Wiltshire, and possibly as many as six other counties were in the hands of men who either then or at some stage of their careers were stewards of the earls concerned.[52] One of the earls, Hugh Bigod, owed his title to Henry II and had possibly held Norfolk and Suffolk only for six months, but the remainder had presumably held office under Stephen.[53] For Stephen's reign as a whole the evidence about sheriffs is fragmentary. Often they were not addressed by name in documents issued by the king; and even when they were named it is hard to know how far he controlled their activities. Support for Stephen was strongest in the east and south-east of the country, and he may have continued to control shrieval administration at least in Norfolk and Suffolk, where for much of his reign the shrievalties were held by the Chesney family.[54] He also may have been reasonably secure in Essex after the downfall of Geoffrey de Mandeville in 1144: Richard de Lucy, a prominent supporter, appears in several documents issued by Stephen as local justiciar preceding the sheriff, Maurice of Tilty, a lesser local man.[55] Knowledge of the justiciars and sheriffs of London (with Middlesex) is reasonably full, but although Stephen's cause was strongly backed by the city, its officers may well have been chosen by the citizens, as Henry I had granted that privilege in 1130 and Stephen is unlikely to have rescinded it.[56] It is possible to identify sheriffs in many counties only at the very end of the reign. The fragmentary evidence both of the identity of sheriffs and of their activity as

royal officials makes inescapable the conclusion that royal control of the office did falter during Stephen's reign.

The sheriff's office thus experienced fluctuating fortunes before 1154. Initially the crown used members of the aristocracy in the localities as ealdormen or earls. The number of earls declined and the nature of their powers altered after the Conquest; it was in the immediate post-Conquest period that the sheriff's power was at its apogee, for as yet his independence was barely affected by the existence of other representatives of royal authority. The growth of central royal government and its extension into the localities from the late eleventh century had begun to affect the sheriff's position by the death of Henry I, but the decline of royal authority under Stephen and the creation of many more earls led to an eclipse of royal control over the shrievalty, until the restoration of peace under a strong king created a climate favourable to the restoration of royal authority in the shires.

Appointments

As information about sheriffs becomes more plentiful it is possible to form an impression of the tempo of change in the office. Between 1066 and 1154 it appears that a change in the ruler was not immediately followed by a purge of sheriffs: even in 1066 English sheriffs were not straightway replaced by Normans. Continuity in local government and revenue collection would have been an important consideration for a new king. Sheriffs' periods of office varied greatly: some served for a matter of months, others for many years. William of Eynesford, for instance, was sheriff of Essex and Hertfordshire for only six months, between Michaelmas 1129 and Easter 1130. At the other extreme, Urse d'Abetot, sheriff of Worcester by 1069, held the county until his death in 1108. A few sheriffs, Urse included, were succeeded by their heirs, but the office did not become generally hereditary.[57]

The early twelfth century stands out as a time of stability in the office, for Henry I tended to keep experienced sheriffs until retirement or death.[58] In the 1120s, however, sheriffs were beginning to come and go at shorter intervals.

One reason may have been growing pressure on the office, but there may also have been a deliberate policy to appoint sheriffs for fixed, relatively short, terms of four or five years, possibly attributable to Roger bishop of Salisbury who was left in charge in England as the king's viceroy between 1123 and 1126. The pipe roll of 1129–30 demonstrates that there was a competitive market for the office: that some men were prepared to pay relatively large sums; that there was no fixed rate for payment; and that payment in itself did not guarantee against dismissal before the full term. That is the only clear evidence that sheriffs did make payments for their office, although it is possible that the fines they were recorded as paying in Domesday Book in connexion with royal manors acted as a precedent. The sums recorded in 1130 were large: Robert d'Oilly, for instance, owed four hundred marks (£226 13s 4d) for Oxfordshire.[59] Some of the less wealthy sheriffs evidently had backers: William of Eynesford, for example, had the backing of Robert of Gloucester to become sheriff of Kent in 1129. That was not altruism on Robert's part but a means of strengthening his influence in a strategically important county where he was already powerful.[60]

Not all the sheriffs newly appointed in 1129–30 had paid for their offices, most notably Richard Basset and Aubrey de Vere, who were appointed joint sheriffs of no fewer than eleven counties, seven at Michaelmas 1129 and the other four at Easter 1130.[61] The reason for their appointment seems to have been financial. There had been an audit of the treasury in the previous financial year, probably because many sheriffs had fallen into arrears with their farms.[62] Changes were made in thirteen or fourteen counties, eleven of which were committed to the two experienced royal agents on special terms, by which they not only acquitted themselves of the farms but paid over a large sum from the profits: 1,000 marks of silver (£666 13s 4d), equivalent approximately to the receipts from two county farms.[63] Such an arrangement was highly unusual although it may not have been entirely without precedent, for Hugh of Buckland is said to have been sheriff of eight counties in 1110.[64] On both occasions the reasons were probably to ensure maximum financial returns from the county farms. In 1110 Henry I had to meet the costs of a treaty with the count of Flanders and the dowry of his eldest daughter, Matilda. Twenty years later Matilda's prospects were still causing concern. By then she was Henry's chosen successor, and her second marriage to the heir of the count of Anjou in 1128 must have been an expensive affair.[65]

Although such large combinations of counties were exceptional, it became customary to hold certain pairs of counties together. The pairing of Nottinghamshire and Derbyshire probably existed in the eleventh century as they shared a county court until 1256.[66] Norfolk and Suffolk was another pairing that went back before the Conquest, although these counties were not always held together. The pairing of Buckinghamshire and Bedfordshire became customary in the twelfth century; Surrey was held with Cambridgeshire and Huntingdonshire in the first half of the twelfth century; and Essex and Hertfordshire were held together under Henry I and then again under Henry II.

The Sheriffs

The earliest certain sheriff on the lists, Wulfsige, was a priest, and the appointment of men who were priests or clerks continued throughout our period. The practice was finally prohibited at the ecclesiastical council of Westminster in 1175 on the grounds that sheriffs might be involved in carrying out judgments involving the shedding of blood.[67] Wulfsige is the only pre-Conquest sheriff known to have been described as a priest, and there is one possibility from the reign of William the Conqueror, Earnwig of Nottinghamshire or Lincolnshire.[68] In the reign of Rufus we are on firmer ground, for Osbert the priest began his long career as a sheriff at that time, first in Lincolnshire and later also in Yorkshire. Little is known of his background other than the comment in the much later chronicle of Meaux abbey that Osbert had been a member of the king's household. He may have been a canon of St Paul's cathedral and a relative of Rannulf Flambard.[69] Hugh of Buckland, whose career began at much the same time as Osbert's, may also have been a canon of St Paul's,[70] which had a close connexion with royal administration in the eleventh and twelfth centuries.[71] In the reign of Henry I there are at least two more clerical sheriffs. First, Richard de Beaumais, formerly a clerk in the household of Roger of Montgomery, became steward of the confiscated Montgomery estates and then acting sheriff of Shropshire, continuing in this role even after his promotion to the see of London.[72] Secondly, Hugh of Leicester, a long-serving sheriff in the midlands, is described in one source as Hugh the priest of Leicester.[73] In the last year covered in the lists, William Comin appears as sheriff of Worcestershire. He is better known as a former chancellor of King David of Scotland who, with David's backing, sought but failed to become bishop of Durham in the 1140s. Subsequently he served in the household of Archbishop Theobald of Canterbury, and then by 1153 he was with Prince Henry's court.[74] In the same year, 1154–5, Richard the sheriff of Wiltshire is probably to be identified as a canon of Salisbury cathedral,[75] and the sheriff of Somerset, Richard of Montacute, possibly with the man of that name who was a chaplain to Stephen's queen, Matilda, and a canon of St Martin le Grand.[76] Clerks as sheriffs had obvious advantages for the crown in that they were presumably literate and could also be rewarded with ecclesiastical preferment which did not directly diminish the king's resources of land.

Most sheriffs, however, were laymen. Laymen of what social degree cannot be established before Domesday Book casts light retrospectively on sheriffs in office on the eve of the Norman Conquest. There they emerge as men of substance in their own shires, but their landed wealth was not on the same scale as that of the earls or the stallers, with one exception. That was Merlosuein of Lincoln whose estates, valued at about £200, put him on a par with the stallers, and like theirs his estates extended through several counties.[77] Other sheriffs were moderately wealthy, like Godric sheriff of Berkshire, whose lands were worth £30 6s.[78] Was that enough to make Godric the richest thegn in Berkshire? It is impossible to know because of the difficulty of distinguishing between pre-Conquest landholders of the same names in Domesday Book.

In the reign of William the Conqueror, however, many sheriffs were extremely wealthy, as is proved by their lands listed in Domesday Book.[79] No fewer than seventeen Norman sheriffs (as well as three survivors from the past) had lands worth more than £100. One, Geoffrey de Mandeville, had lands worth almost £800, and another five had lands worth between £400 and £650. Some sheriffs had evidently been given large estates more or less at the time they were appointed. William Malet, for example, was sheriff of Yorkshire for a short period only in 1069, yet Domesday Book records him as being in possession of large estates.[80] They fall into three groups: first, those to the west and east of York itself, within easy reach of the castle and clustered round the Roman road leading from York to Tadcaster and on into the West Riding; second, the estate at Stokesley with its dependent holdings, situated between the northern slopes of the North York Moors and the river Tees; and third, the estates in Holderness strung out along the east coast. Yorkshire was a dangerous place for the Normans in 1068 and 1069, for they were challenged both by the local population and by Danish invaders. William Malet in his outpost at York was provided with a substantial landed base from which to extend Norman rule.

A similar case could be made out for some of the other wealthy sheriffs. Geoffrey de Mandeville, for instance, was granted the lands of Ansger the staller. According to the *Carmen de Hastingae Proelio*, Ansger organized the defence of London against King William in 1066, and it appears as though Geoffrey was in charge of the city as early as 1067.[81] Other sheriffs, however, acquired their great wealth over a period of years. Most of the richest men in the Conqueror's England had close ties to Duke William, and many were already rich in Normandy. A striking exception is Roger Bigod, one of the richest men in England in 1086 and yet, so far as it is possible to discover, of only moderate wealth in Normandy. He may well have owed his initial good fortune in England to Odo of Bayeux, whose tenant he had been in Normandy and from whom he held land in England.[82] Not long after 1066 Roger appears as sheriff of Norfolk, and he soon began to accumulate estates. He had acquired land in Norfolk in the time of Archbishop Stigand, who fell in 1071;[83] he also profited in Norfolk and Suffolk from the fall of Earl Ralph in 1075,[84] and acquired estates initially given to William Malet.[85] Roger evidently impressed the king as a reliable man, for as well as Norfolk he also held Suffolk as sheriff for two terms before 1086, and he held many royal estates at farm. His estates, like those of William Malet in Yorkshire, were thickly concentrated along the coast in a way that suggests concern about coastal defence. Roger is thus a supreme example of a man who was in the right place at the right time, and made the fortunes of his family as a result.

By no means all William's sheriffs were men of such wealth. For example, the sheriff of Surrey in 1086 was Ranulf, whose only recorded property in that county was a house in Guildford which he held of the bishop of Bayeux.[86] The varied status of William's sheriffs reflects different considerations in appointments. On some occasions the king evidently did appoint men with large estates who had power locally to carry through the Norman settlement, but that did not become a general policy. It was not always possible, for in parts of the country much land was in the hands of the church, and sheriffs had to pick up what they could by fair means or foul. Urse d'Abetot, for instance, was appointed as sheriff of Worcestershire shortly after 1066, but much land in the county was held by the bishop of Worcester and the abbeys of Evesham and Westminster. Although Urse acquired a moderate tenancy-in-chief, the majority of his estates were obtained as under-tenancies, sometimes by dubious methods which gave him an evil reputation as a despoiler of the church.[87]

It would appear, moreover, that the Conqueror did not want to create a class of sheriffs who combined great local wealth with control of local government in a way that would have been difficult to control. He had already had experience of the kind of problems that could arise before he came to England. The *vicomtes* of western Normandy, ducal officials roughly comparable with sheriffs, were powerful local magnates who had taken a leading part in the revolt against William in 1046–7.[88] Yet in the great distribution of land that took place in England after 1066, sheriffs were well placed to profit, and the king was not disposed to curb their activities too strictly.

After the reign of William the Conqueror sheriffs generally were men of more moderate standing, although individual magnates continued to be appointed to the office throughout the period.[89] Rufus and Henry I may well have been motivated by reluctance to allow magnates too much local power, reluctance that was well founded, as Stephen's experiences were to prove. Men of moderate standing often held land of greater lords, who obviously had a strong incentive for having sheriffs as under-tenants. Osbert the priest and Hugh of Buckland are far from isolated examples of sheriffs who picked up undertenancies. Some sheriffs held land of more than one lord;[90] others were more closely tied to the interests of particular magnates, whose wishes they would have found hard to resist. In Henry I's reign William Peverel, for instance, was the overlord of three sheriffs of Nottinghamshire,[91] and two sheriffs of Devon were under-tenants of the Redvers family.[92]

The Norman kings were not averse from appointing as sheriffs men closely associated with their own courts – curial sheriffs as they are usually known. This description disguises links with the court of differing kinds and degree. Some sheriffs held offices in the household before or during their terms as sheriffs; other were men who, without holding formal office, were evidently closely associated with the king, perhaps as knights of his household, and were given local lands and estates. Those who held formal offices in the household are easiest to detect, and throughout the Norman period there were always a few sheriffs who combined local office with stewardships, constableships, or chamberlainships at court. Two sheriffs in Rufus's reign, Roger Bigod and Ivo Taillebois, were both royal stewards.[93] The shrievalties of Gloucestershire and Worcestershire came to be associated with the custody of Gloucester and Worcester castles and with constableships of the court.[94] A powerful combination of offices was held by William de Pont de l'Arche, who was sheriff of Hampshire for many years in Henry I's reign, and who in 1120 was also given custody of the treasury at Winchester, holding both posts at least until the end of the reign.[95] Henry I also used as sheriffs men who had been members of his military household and had been given local estates, such as Thomas of St John in Oxfordshire and Rualon d'Avranches in Kent.[96] Usually there were only a few *curiales* in office at any one time: the exception was 1130 when Richard Basset and Aubrey de

Vere were appointed joint sheriffs of eleven counties, and that arrangement, as we have seen, was exceptional.

Notwithstanding the need for contact between government at the centre and in the localities, the office continued to be filled by men with local interests. From the time details survive about sheriffs' estates, it is evident that many were local men, even if the size of their estates varied greatly. The Norman kings could and did move sheriffs to counties where they had little or no land, but not so frequently as to provoke the kind of protests against the practice that were voiced in the Provisions of Oxford of 1258.[97]

One important development that may be detected in appointments is the rise of sheriffs experienced in administration. The earliest signs come in the reign of William Rufus with the careers of Osbert the priest and Hugh of Buckland who both became effectively professional sheriffs, men who made their careers in the shires rather than in the itinerant royal household. Others rose to join them in the early twelfth century, such as Gilbert the knight, he of cheerful demeanour at the Exchequer, or Hugh of Leicester. Henry I kept sheriffs he trusted for many years, not so much switching them from county to county as adding extra counties to the ones they already held.

Hugh of Leicester already had administrative experience when he came to the shrievalty, for he had been steward to Matilda de Senlis.[98] He was not the only sheriff to be recruited from honorial administration. In the reign of Henry I there are three other cases: Anschetil of Bulmer was or had been the steward of Robert Fossard; Ansfrid the sheriff was probably Ansfrid steward of the archbishop of Canterbury; and Richard de Beaumais had been a clerk in the household of Roger of Montgomery.[99] As already mentioned, at the end of Stephen's reign several counties were accounted for by men who are known at some stage of their careers to have been earls' stewards. In that way the general growth of government in the twelfth century, both royal and baronial, produced an increasing number of men with administrative experience whom the crown could employ as sheriffs.

The sheriff's office was not only powerful, it was highly profitable, as is shown by the payments sheriffs were prepared to offer to hold the office in the 1120s. The system of farming the king's lands and rights meant that any profits went to the sheriff. By the twelfth century sheriffs also enjoyed partial exemption from danegeld, and they had begun to collect a tax on their own account, sheriff's aid.[100] In addition to those privileges there were other less legitimate profits of office. In the Norman period it was evidently not unknown for sheriffs to call shire and hundred courts more frequently than at the customary intervals, presumably increasing their revenues from fines, for Henry I issued an ordinance forbidding the practice.[101] According to Domesday Book, sheriffs had disposed of parcels of land belonging to royal manors: in the case of one in Buckinghamshire the beneficiary had been a girl who taught the sheriff's daughter orphrey work (gold embroidery).[102] The charges brought against Restold, a former sheriff of Oxfordshire, in 1130 included taking away villeins and burgesses from royal manors.[103]

The misdeeds of sheriffs are a recurring theme in eleventh and twelfth century sources. For Heming, historian of the church of Worcester, there was little to choose between Aevic, sheriff under Cnut, and the notorious Urse d'Abetot as predators on that church.[104] William the Conqueror sought to make sheriffs give back lands they had taken from the church,[105] and doubtless the most flagrant abuses were eventually corrected, but sheriffs were still a cause for complaint at the beginning of Stephen's reign. Stephen's second Charter of Liberties promised to remedy 'all exactions, injustices and 'miskennings' imposed by sheriffs or others'.[106] Appointments to the office were a cause of anxiety at the end of the reign, for one account of the treaty between Stephen and Henry in 1153 stated that sheriffs should be appointed who would not abuse their influence.[107]

A sheriff's career could end in debt and obscurity, as was the fate of Restold, but for the fortunate it could be the making of a family's prosperity, not simply through the office itself but also through the further opportunities opened up for acquiring land, for arranging advantageous marriages for sons and daughters, or for securing advancement for sons in the church. For example, Dr Walker has traced the history of the hereditary sheriffs of Gloucestershire, showing how their originally modest estates were augmented by two marriages, first that of Miles of Gloucester to the daughter and heiress of Bernard de Neufmarché, and, second, that of Miles's son and heir Roger to the daughter of Payn FitzJohn; Miles himself was created earl of Hereford by the Empress.[108] There is no evidence for the pre-Conquest period, but certainly service to the crown after 1066 was the most important avenue for social advancement open to laymen, and the office of sheriff brought with it both local influence and the possibility of royal patronage.

The Lists

Sheriffs may easily be identified from pipe rolls after 1154, but for the preceding period lists have to be constructed from a range of sources. The most readily available lists for all counties hitherto have been those in *List of Sheriffs for England and Wales from the Earliest Times to AD 1831* (*Lists and Indexes* IX), originally published in 1896 and reprinted in 1963 with amendments made by Mabel Mills to the copy which was kept in the Round Room of the Public Record Office at Chancery Lane.[109] The amendments incorporated work by individual scholars in the early twentieth century on individual counties, notably by Farrer, Round, and Hunter Blair, or on particular sources, principally by Curtis Walker on the 1130 pipe roll.[110] Yet even in their revised form the lists are of limited usefulness. The range of sources consulted was too narrow, periods of office were sometimes dated with greater confidence than the sources allow, and in general more discussion of the candidates and the evidence should have been included. The lists which follow here are thus more detailed than those in *Lists and Indexes* IX, and they include references derived from charters and cartularies, many still unpublished. The underlying approach to sources has nevertheless been critical. The aim has been to supply references to those whom there is good reason to think were sheriffs rather than to list all conceivable possibilities.

The material has been arranged in three columns. In the first appears the name of the sheriff, preceded by a question mark if there is doubt whether or not he was a sheriff of the county concerned. One problem that arose was how many of the early references to include to men known to have been reeves but whose sphere of influence is uncertain. It was decided only to include the more probable candidates, omitting those royal reeves who were not clearly in charge of shires.[111] Entries have been placed in diamond brackets if an individual has been suggested as a sheriff without corroborative evidence, as has been found with some of the emendations to *Lists and Indexes* IX. No attempt has been made to standardize variant spellings of forenames: 'Ranulf' and 'Rannulf', for instance, may refer to different men. 'Surnames' which represent identifiable place-names have, so far as is possible, been rendered in their modern form with the particle in the appropriate language; otherwise they are cited as they appear in manuscript form. In the second column dates of tenure are given where known; more commonly the dates are those of occurrence, or covering dates of documents in which sheriffs occur. The third column contains the sources, three of which threw up questions of methodology requiring some discussion here.

First, there are royal writs and charters. They are difficult to date precisely and in most cases the dates given in the lists are covering dates.[112] In the case of writs, it is also not always straightforward to establish which of the individuals addressed, if any, were sheriffs. The address clauses of pre-Conquest writs might include stallers, as we have already seen, or others addressed simply by name, and unless there were other grounds for believing such men were sheriffs, they have not been included.[113] Under the Norman kings also writs might be addressed to laymen other than sheriffs. Sometimes addressees were local magnates, as in the case of Robert de Lacy in Yorkshire in the early years of Henry I's reign,[114] or men directly concerned in the subject matter of the document, for example Walter de Gant addressed in a notification issued by Henry I.[115] Sometimes addressees were acting as royal justiciars.[116] Furthermore, documents issued by the Norman kings were sometimes addressed to X the sheriff without specifying his county, or X the sheriff of Y county where X is identified only by his initial.[117] In the former cases the lists indicate where, although the county is not explicitly mentioned, it may be identified from the context of the document. In the latter cases the possibility of more than one sheriff with the initial R, for example, has been borne in mind, and separate entries have usually been made.[118]

Secondly, Domesday Book identifies a number of individuals as sheriffs both before and after 1066. Sometimes men living in 1086 were not always sheriffs in all counties in which they are mentioned. For example, Aiulf the sheriff occurs in the Domesday survey of Berkshire. There is no evidence that he was sheriff of that county in 1086, but he was sheriff of Dorset then. However, as it is not clear who was sheriff of Berkshire in 1086, Aiulf has to be considered as a candidate, and consequently appears in the Berkshire list with a query before his name. Sometimes men are not described as sheriffs but had evidently been holding royal manors at farm, a task which sheriffs often performed, and they also appear in the lists with a query before their names.

Thirdly, there is the pipe roll evidence, chiefly that of the 1130 pipe roll. A sheriff in office, say from Michaelmas 1129 to Michaelmas 1130, was described in the 1130 pipe roll as accounting for the farm of a particular county. He may have been in office only for half of the year, either from Michaelmas to Easter or Easter to Michaelmas, and this short tenure was recorded. The term 'old farm' was used of arrears, entered either before the farm for the year just ended, or after it. If more than one sheriff had debts outstanding, the arrears from 1128–1129 were entered before those for 1127–1128. The payments recorded in the 1130 pipe roll for sheriffs to hold their offices for fixed terms of four or five years also help to establish their dates in office.[119]

The extracts made from the roll for 1154 to 1155 and the roll for the following year have been used for the information they contain about sheriffs in the closing years of Stephen's reign, but, as will be seen in the lists, it is not always easy to decide whether certain individuals were sheriffs or perhaps under-sheriffs. The lists draw attention to men who, whilst described as sheriffs, may have been under-sheriffs. Little is known about under-sheriffs in this period but they must have been employed in cases where a single man was sheriff of several counties.[120]

Some counties came customarily to be held as a pair by a single sheriff, as already mentioned, but as it cannot be assumed that the pairings were stable, all counties are listed separately with references to pairings.

Finally, mention must be made of the administrative geography underlying the lists. Throughout the period under review Rutland and Westmorland were not constituted as shires;[121] accordingly they do not appear. Cumberland was a late developer, but as 'Carlisle' it appears in the 1130 pipe roll, and has been included as a marginal case.[122] In a few other counties, although sheriffs do appear after the Norman Conquest, they were not in every case royal officials, for great magnates began to appoint their own sheriffs.[123] The sheriffs of Cheshire and Durham were controlled by the earl and the bishop respectively; the only sheriff known to have acted in Lancashire was evidently the officer of Roger of Poitou; and Northumberland, Shropshire, and Sussex had royal sheriffs for only part of the period. Attention has been drawn at the appropriate points to the status as royal or baronial officials of the sheriffs listed.

Notes

1 For a brief survey see Stenton, *Anglo-Saxon England*, pp. 336–8.
2 Taylor, *Gloucestershire Studies*, pp. 17–51; Mahany and Roffe, *Anglo-Norman Studies*, V (1983), 197–219; Roffe, *Landscape History*, III (1982), 27–36; Roffe, *Derbyshire Archaeological Journal*, CVI (1986), 102–22.
3 For a description of political divisions in the north see Kapelle, *Norman Conquest of the North*, ch. 1; also Whitelock, in *The Anglo-Saxons*, pp. 70–88.
4 *ASChs.*, no. 77; *Hemingi Chartularium*, I, 277, 278.
5 For example, *ASC s.a.* 1001 (A), 1002 (C, D, E). Loyn drew attention to the career of the royal reeve Wulfstan of Dalham, Cambs, described in the *Liber Eliensis*: *British Government and Administration*, p. 11. Morris collected references to reeves: *Medieval English Sheriff*, pp. 1–16. See also Campbell in *Domesday Studies: Papers Read at the Novocentenary Conference*, pp. 201–18.
6 *Charters of Rochester*, nos. 34, 69.
7 Morris, *Medieval English Sheriff*, pp. 20–1.
8 For the text of the Ordinance in translation:

English Historical Documents, I, *c. 500–1042*, 429–30.

9 Loyn, in *British Government and Administration*, p. 13; Cam, *EHR*, XLVII (1932), 353–76.

10 See articles by Roffe cited n. 2 above.

11 Loyn, in *British Government and Administration*, pp. 6–7.

12 Keynes, *Diplomas of King Aethelred*, p. 198; for a general assessment of the political context: Stafford, in *Ethelred the Unready*, pp. 15–46.

13 The work of Round and subsequent scholars in reconstructing hundredal assessments has shown that by the eleventh century the geld must have been assigned to the county and then distributed between the hundreds: see Round, *Feudal England*, p. 83.

14 Harmer, *Anglo-Saxon Writs*, introduction, especially pp. 34–5, 45–54.

15 Loyn, *Governance of Anglo-Saxon England*, pp. 140–8; Morris, *Medieval English Sheriff*, pp. 24–5, 88–94, where it is assumed, probably correctly, that the sheriff had jurisdiction over crown pleas, and that this area of responsibility was taken over by royal justices in the twelfth century.

16 *Leges Edwardi Confessoris*, c. 28, 1.

17 Morris, *The Frankpledge System*, ch. 4; *Leges Henrici Primi*, c. 8, 1.

18 Green, *EHR*, XCVI (1981), 241–58.

19 Green, *Government of England*, pp. 55–69.

20 Stafford, *Economic History Review*, 2nd Series, XXXIII (1980), 491–502.

21 *DB*, I, 299.

22 Green, *Government of England*, pp. 63–4.

23 Morris, *Medieval English Sheriff*, pp. 96–7.

24 *DB*, I, 252, 179; Morris, *Medieval English Sheriff*, p. 27. For the pre-Conquest hundred and military service, see John, *Bulletin of the John Rylands Library*, XLVI (1963), 14–41.

25 *ASC s.a.* 1056.

26 Hollister, *Anglo-Saxon Military Institutions*, pp. 94–5.

27 Green, *Government of England*, p. 120.

28 Green, *Government of England*, pp. 122–4.

29 John in *Anglo-Saxon England*, p. 237.

30 Caenegem, *Royal Writs in England from the Conquest to Glanvill*, p. 129.

31 Stenton, *Anglo-Saxon England*, pp. 398, 414–16; Keynes, *Diplomas of King Aethelred*, pp. 197–8; Freeman, *History of the Norman Conquest*, II, App. G.

32 In Domesday Book Orgar, King Edward's sheriff of Cambridgeshire, was said later (probably therefore after he had ceased to be sheriff) to have been Ansger the Staller's man: *DB*, I, 197b. Mr P. Wormald kindly drew my attention to this point.

33 There are references in Domesday Book to the earl's third penny of the county in Dorset and Warwick: *DB*, I, 75, 238, and to the third penny of hundreds in Hampshire and Devon: *DB*, I, 38b, 101. For the earl's third penny in general, see *Complete Peerage*, IV, App. H, pp. 657–62; Round, *Geoffrey de Mandeville*, p. 287.

34 For texts see Harmer, nos. 75, 77, 84, 85, 91, 98, and the spurious texts nos. 76, 93.

35 For a recent discussion of the subject see Mack, *Journal of Medieval History*, XII (1986), 123–35. It is worth pointing out that the reference in *DB* to Robert FitzWymarc, King Edward's staller, holding the shrievalty of Essex was concerned with an incident which occurred after the arrival of King William, *DB*, II, 98.

36 *ASC s.a.* 1072 (*recte* 1071).

37 *Complete Peerage*, IX, 703–6.

38 Douglas, *William the Conqueror*, pp. 294–6.

39 For Shropshire see Mason, *Transactions of the Shropshire Archaeological Society*, LVI (1957–60), 244–7.

40 *Complete Peerage*, XII(1), 493–5; XII(2), 357–60; VI, 640–1; II, 386–7; VII, 523–6; V, 683–6.

41 The only clear example between 1066 and 1100 is *RRAN*, I, no. 388 (Warwick). There are more examples from Henry I's reign: *RRAN*, II, nos. 639 (Warenne), 654, 1151 (Warwick), 509, 607, 650, 732, 743, 744, 770, 929, 966, 967, 996, 1064, 1066, 1359 (Huntingdon).

42 Green, *Government of England*, pp. 107–10 and references there cited.

43 *Dialogus de Scaccario*, p. 7.

44 Green, *Government of England*, pp. 40–50, and references there cited.

45 Colker, *Studia Monastica*, XII (1970), 260.

46 *Dialogus de Scaccario*, pp. 36–43, for a description of the various methods of surcharging. For comment see Green, *Government of England*, p. 63.

47 *Dialogus de Scaccario*, p. 50.

48 White, 'The Restoration of Order in England 1153–4', ch. 4; Amt, 'From Tempus Werre to Pax Publica', ch. 6.

49 Viz Ansfrid in Kent, and possibly Warin in one or more of his counties of Dorset, Somerset and Wiltshire, Fulk in Cambridgeshire, Huntingdonshire and Surrey, and William de Pont de l'Arche in Hampshire.

50 Davis, *King Stephen*, app. I; Latimer, *Bulletin of the Institute of Historical Research*, LIX (1986), 137–45.

51 Davis, *King Stephen*, pp. 131–2.
52 *RBE*, II, 649, 651–2, 653. The six counties in the hands of stewards were Herefordshire (Maurice), Gloucestershire (Osbert of Westbury), Nottinghamshire and Derbyshire (Robert de Perer), Northamptonshire (Robert Grimbald), and Leicestershire (Geoffrey l'Abbé). Maurice attested a charter of Roger earl of Hereford as steward: *Charters of the Earldom of Hereford*, no. 43, p. 31; Osbert as steward of the same earl: nos. 27, p. 25, no. 36, p. 36; Robert de Perer was steward of Robert de Ferrers, earl of Derby: *Hatton's Book of Seals*, p. 104; Robert Grimbald attests as steward of Simon de Senlis earl of Northampton: BL Royal MS 11 B IX, f. 12, see also Farrer, *Honors and Knights Fees*, II, 302; Crouch suggests Geoffrey l'Abbé was appointed steward before 1163, possibly as a result of his losing the shrievalty of Leicestershire: Crouch, *Beaumont Twins*, p. 142.
53 *Cartae Antiquae Rolls 11–20*, no. 553, pp. 157–8.
54 Robert FitzWalter, who had been sheriff of the two counties in Henry I's reign, was an under-tenant of Stephen's honour of Eye: *RBE*, I, 411; Round, *EHR*, XXXV (1920), 493. He was succeeded as sheriff by his sons John and William, both of whom received land from Stephen: *RRAN*, III, nos. 174–177. Towards the end of Stephen's reign the family lost the two counties, but William's successor in Norfolk, Roger Gulafre, probably also came from a family holding land of the honour of Eye. In 1166 Philip Gulafre held four fees of the honour: *RBE*, I, 411.
55 *RRAN*, III, 544–50, 552, 559.
56 Reynolds, *History*, LVII (1972), 342–3; Brooke and Keir, *London*, pp. 213–218; Brooke, Keir, and Reynolds, *Journal of the Society of Archivists*, IV (1973), 558–78, discuss the concessions Henry I and Stephen made to the city.
57 Green, *Anglo-Norman Studies*, V, 131–2.
58 Green, *Government of England*, pp. 155–6.
59 *PR 31 Henry I*, p. 2. These payments are discussed in Green, *Government of England*, pp. 201–4.
60 *PR 31 Henry I*, p. 65; Green, *Government of England*, pp. 202, 212.
61 *PR 31 Henry I*, pp. 43–4, 52–3, 81, 90, 100. The appointments of Richard and Aubrey are discussed in Green, *Government of England*, pp. 47, 65–6, 204.
62 Green, *Government of England*, pp. 47, 93, 204.
63 *PR 31 Henry I*, p. 63.
64 *Chron. Abingdon*, II, 117; Brooke and Keir, *London*, p. 206.
65 Morris, *Medieval English Sheriff*, pp. 78–9; Green, *Government of England*, pp. 199–200.
66 Crook, *Derbyshire Archaeological Journal*, CIII (1983), 98–106; Roffe, *Derbyshire Archaeological Journal*, CVI (1986), 102–22.
67 *Councils and Synods with other documents relating to the English Church*, I(2), 985.
68 No tenant-in-chief called Earnwig occurs in 1086 but Ernuin the priest occurs in Nottinghamshire, Lincolnshire, and Lancashire: *DB*, I, 293, 330b, 331, 336b, 347, 371, 374, 376.
69 *Chron. Melsa*, I, 86; trans. Bird, *Genealogist*, new series, XXXII (1916), 154; Le Neve, *Fasti*, I, 43.
70 Le Neve, *Fasti*, I, 51; Brooke and Keir, *London*, p. 204.
71 Brooke and Keir, *London*, pp. 344–9.
72 Mason, *Transactions of the Shropshire Archaeological Society*, LVI (1957–60), 253–4.
73 An account of the case of Abbot Gunter of Thorney (1085–1112) over land at Charwelton before the leading men of Northamptonshire and Leicestershire records the presence of Hugh the priest, sheriff of Northampton: CUL Additional MS 3020, f. 414v.
74 Young, *William Cumin: Border Politics and the Bishopric of Durham 1141–1144*, p. 26.
75 *Sarum Charters*, p. 19; I owe this reference to Dr. D.E. Greenway. Richard was presumably the same Richard the clerk, sheriff of Wiltshire, appointed in 1160: *PR 7 Henry II*, p. 8.
76 *RRAN*, III, nos. 23, 503, 655, 991; Davis, *London Topographical Record*, XXIII (1974 for 1972), 20; see *Complete Peerage*, IX, 75 for an alternative identification.
77 *DB*, I, 86, 95, 95b, 113b, 121b, 122, 122b, 124b, 298, 298b, 313, 325b, 326, 362b, 363, 374. This is a higher estimate than that by Mack: *Journal of Medieval History*, XII (1986), 127.
78 *DB*, I, 58, 60b. Godric had also appropriated parcels of royal manors: *DB*, I, 57b.
79 Green, *Anglo-Norman Studies*, V, 131–2.
80 Green, *Anglo-Norman Studies*, V, 142.
81 *Carmen de Hastingae Proelio*, pp. 44–5; *RRAN*, I, nos. 15, 265 and list for London and Middlesex below for comment; Brooke and Keir, *London*, pp. 191–200.
82 Loyd, *Anglo-Norman Families*, pp. 14–15.
83 *DB*, II, 139 (Earsham), 173 (soke at Flitcham).
84 e.g. *DB*, II, 185b (Stoke Holy Cross, Norf), 333 (Bulcamp, Suff), 335 (Ellough, Suff).
85 e.g. *DB*, II, 332b (Chediston), 333 (Thorpe, Halesworth).
86 *DB*, I, 30.
87 Green, *Anglo-Norman Studies*, V, 144.
88 William of Poitiers, *Gesta Guillelmi*, pp. 14–20,

Pain steward of Honour of Huntingdon (Chrs of David I no. 76) may have been Pain of Hemingford, sheriff of Cambridge, Hunts and Surrey (see below passim).

21

and for the office of *vicomte*: Haskins, *Norman Institutions*, pp. 41–7. There is a good recent study of the office in eastern Normandy by Bouvris in *Autour du pouvoir ducal normand Xᵉ-XIIᵉ siècles*, pp. 149–74.

89 For William II's reign see Barlow, *William Rufus*, pp. 188–9. Examples from the reign of Henry I include Richard FitzBaldwin (Devon), Robert d'Oilly (Oxon), Aubrey de Vere (eleven counties): Green, *Government of England*, pp. 210, 264–5, 276. In Stephen's reign some earls held shrievalties themselves, or the sheriffs seem to have been their subordinates, see above, p. 13.

90 For examples from Henry I's reign, see Green, *Government of England*, pp. 238 (Bertram of Bulmer), 247 (William of Eynesford).

91 Green, *Government of England*, p. 211.

92 For Geoffrey de Mandeville and Geoffrey de Furneaux, see Green, *Government of England*, pp. 197, 255; Bearman, 'Charters of the Redvers Family and the Earldom of Devon in the Twelfth Century', pp. 136–8, 148–9.

93 *RRAN*, I, no. 391.

94 Morris, *Medieval English Sheriff*, pp. 50–1.

95 Green, *Government of England*, especially pp. 267–8.

96 Green, *Government of England*, pp. 147–8, 271–2. On rewards given to knights of the household: Prestwich, *EHR*, XCVI (1981), 1–35.

97 *Documents of the Baronial Movement of Reform and Rebellion 1258–67*, p. 108. The use of such men as sheriffs is discussed by Carpenter, *EHR*, XCI (1976), pp. 28–9.

98 *Mon. Ang.*, V, 178.

99 *RRAN*, II, no. 1627 (Anschetil of Bulmer); Green, *Government of England*, p. 205 (Ansfrid); Mason, *Transactions of the Shropshire Archaeological Society*, LVI (1957–60), 253–4 (Richard de Beaumais).

100 Green, *Government of England*, pp. 172–3.

101 *Select Charters*, p. 122.

102 *DB*, I, 149b.

103 *PR 31 Henry I*, p. 2.

104 *Hemingi Chartularium*, I, 254, 264, 269, 277.

105 *English Historical Documents*, II, no. 38, p. 463.

106 *Select Charters*, p. 144.

107 *Radulfi de Diceto Decani Lundoniensis Opera Historica*, I, 297.

108 Walker, *Transactions of the Bristol and Gloucestershire Archaeological Society*, LXXVII (1958), 66–96.

109 Lists of sheriffs are also to be found in *DK Report 31*, App. 3 (for Cheshire) and 4 (for other English counties).

110 Farrer, *EHR*, XXX (1915), 277–85; Round, *EHR*, XXXV (1920), 481–96; Blair, *Archaeologia Aeliana*, 4th series, XX (1942), 11–91; XXII (1944), 22–82; Walker, *EHR* XXXVII (1922), 67–79; references to other useful lists are cited under the appropriate county.

111 Such reeves who, for want of a better description, might be described as proto-sheriffs include:
(1) Wulfstan of Dalham, a man close to King Eadred, who held courts of more than one hundred, and another at Cambridge: *LE*, pp. 93–4, 116, and for comment p. xiii.
(2) Eadric, who was described as holding a royal court at Calne in Wiltshire in the miracles of St Swithun: *Frithegodi Monachi Breuiloquium Vitae Beati Wilfredi et Wulfstani Cantoris Narratio Metrica de Sancto Swithuno*, 11, 299–307.
(3) Aelfgar the king's reeve present at a meeting of the shire court at Cuckamsley, Berks in Aethelred's reign: *ASChs*, no. 76.
(4) Ufegeat the shireman who witnessed a bequest recorded in a (spurious) will of Ethelred's reign: Whitelock, *Anglo-Saxon Wills*, no. 22. I owe references (2) to (4) to Mr P. Wormald.

112 The dates given in *RRAN*, I, have been accepted unless revised subsequently by other scholars. The editors of volume two gave covering dates and where possible suggested more precise dates of issue. As the latter were somewhat speculative, it was decided to refer to the covering dates of documents cited.

113 For a general discussion of those addressed in royal writs, see Harmer, pp. 45–54. Three men occur in the address clauses of pre-Conquest writs who may have been sheriffs, but have been excluded from the list as there is no evidence about their status: Kineward (Berks), Wada (Devon), and Kinric (Hunts): Harmer, nos. 3, 120, 57, 58. Richard who is addressed in no. 117 is described in no. 118 as the king's housecarl, and Harmer suggested that he may have been Richard son of Scrob. Aethelric was addressed in nos. 29, and 30, but in no. 26 he follows Aethelwine the shire-man and it seems more likely that the latter was sheriff. For the stallers see above n. 34. The counties and stallers concerned are Middlesex (Osgod Clapa and Ansger), Essex (Robert FitzWymarc and Ansger), Hampshire (Eadnoth), Hertfordshire (Ansger), together with London (Ansger).

114 *RRAN*, II, nos. 496, 559, 598.

115 *RRAN*, II, no. 1097, and see discussion under Lincolnshire.

116 It was argued by Round that as a local justiciar

sometimes preceded a sheriff in the address clauses of royal documents, especially in Stephen's reign, the order of precedence could be used to determine which of two men was the justiciar and which the sheriff in documents where offices were not mentioned: *Commune of London*, p. 109. Cronne basically accepted Round's argument, although cautiously: *University of Birmingham Historical Journal*, VI (1957–8), 24. Local justiciars before 1135 are rarely referred to in strictly contemporary sources: Green, *Government of England*, pp. 107–8.

117 For example, *RRAN*, II, nos. 550, 997; I, no. 212.

118 For example, see list for Surrey.

119 Although references to arrears of the farm are usually entered near the start of the sheriff's account, there are occasional references to old debts at other points in the 1130 pipe roll, viz those of Aiulf, Serlo de Burg, and William of Buckland: *PR 31 Henry I*, pp. 14, 31, 127.

120 Green, *Government of England*, pp. 120, 121.

121 The position of Westmorland was summarized succinctly by Holt, *The Northerners*, p. 199. For the early history of Rutland: Adams, *Mercian Studies*, pp. 63–84; *VCH Rutland*, I, 165–71.

122 In 1130 account was made for the revenues of 'Carlisle' by Hildret, whose office was not specified. There are entries under the Carlisle heading for debts of Odard the sheriff 'for the old farm for the pleas of Carlisle which belong to the shrievalty', for the same farm for the previous year (i.e. 1128–1129), and for the pleas of W[alter] Espec and Eustace FitzJohn: *PR 31 Henry I*, p. 142. Odard the sheriff was perhaps the man called Odard who was sheriff of Northumberland in 1129–1130, and, if so, it would appear therefore that he had had some authority over Carlisle: *PR 31 Henry I*, p. 35.

123 On baronial sheriffs, see Stenton, *The First Century of English Feudalism 1066–1166*, pp. 67–8.

Bedfordshire

Aelfstan	1053 × 1066	Occurs as witness to a charter of Oswulf and Aethelith for St Albans abbey: Fowler, *Bedfordshire Historical Record Society*, V (1920), 55 = S 1235.
? Godric	before 1066	A man of Godric the sheriff held land in Bedfordshire: *DB*, I, 213. There is no indication from the entry that Godric had been sheriff of this county, but he had been sheriff of Berkshire and possibly Buckinghamshire.
Ralph Taillebois	1066 × 1086	Living 1075 × 1081: *LE*, p. 196; but dead by 1086: *DB*, I, 218, 218b.
? Ivo Taillebois	1066 × 1086	Imposed an increment on the farm of a royal manor before 1086, and so was either sheriff or farmer of royal land: *DB*, I, 209b.
? Hugh de Beauchamp	1070 × 1089	Writ of King William addressed to Peter of Valognes, Hugh de Beauchamp, and all his sheriffs, protecting the seisin of St Albans abbey in all its lands. Peter was probably addressed here as sheriff of Hertfordshire and Hugh as sheriff of Buckinghamshire, but as the abbey had a claim to land in Bedfordshire held by Hugh in 1086 (*DB*, I, 213) he could have been sheriff of this county also: Matthew Paris, *Chronica Majora*, VI, 34 (not in *RRAN*, I).
? Hugh of Buckland	1087 × 1097 1100 × 1115	*RRAN*, I, no. 395; II, nos. 812, 957, 960. Hugh was living in 1115 but dead before 1118: *RRAN*, II, nos. 1102, 1180.
? Richard of Winchester	before 1125	Daughter accounts for old farm: *PR 31 Henry I*, p. 100.
Maenfenin	1125–1129	Accounts for old farm and for holding Bedfordshire and Buckinghamshire for four years: *PR 31 Henry I*, p. 100; *RRAN*, II, no. 1505.
Richard Basset and Aubrey de Vere	1129–1130	*PR 31 Henry I*, p. 100.
William Bacon	1135 × 1154	*RRAN*, III, no. 683; still living 1159 × 1161: PRO DL 25/68, calendared *DK Report 35*, App., p. 8.
William	1148 × 1160, poss. 1148 × 1155	*Chron. Ram.* I, 308 = *English Episcopal Acta*, I, no. 225, p. 142 (date based on comments by editor of latter); presumably to be identified with William Bacon.

Berkshire

Godric	before 1066	Reported to have been killed at battle of Hastings: *DB*, I, 57b; Harmer, no. 5; *Chron. Abingdon*, I, 485. Cf. *DB*, I, 60b, where it is implied that Godric survived the battle.
? Henry de Ferrers	after 1066	Succeeded to the lands held by Godric the sheriff TRE, including parcels of land belonging to royal manors: *DB* I, 57b. There is no other evidence that Henry was sheriff, but as Godric was killed at Hastings and his lands were presumably soon redistributed, Henry may have taken over his office as well as his lands.
Froger	1066 × 1086, prob. soon after 1066	*DB*, I, 57b; *Chron. Abingdon*, I, 486–7; II, 117.
? Robert d'Oilly and/or Roger de Pîtres	c. 1071	Addressed in *RRAN*, I, no. 49, a writ confirming Abingdon abbey in all its lands, which were in Berkshire, Oxfordshire, Gloucestershire, and Warwickshire. Robert was possibly sheriff of Oxfordshire and Warwickshire and Roger of Gloucestershire, and they may have been addressed in those capacities, but either or both could have been sheriff of Berkshire.
? Aiulf	1086	*DB*, I, 63, possibly in his capacity as sheriff of Dorset or Somerset.
? Gilbert de Brettevilla	1090 × 1094	*RRAN*, I, no. 359.
Hugh of Buckland	1097, 1100 × 1110, poss. not continuously, see next entry	*Chron. Abingdon*, II, 43; *RRAN*, II, nos. 528, 550 (1101 × 1102), 615 (1102, 1103, 1107 or 1109), 695 (1100 × 1107), 703 (1101 × 1105), 721 (1100 × 1105), 736, 854 (1100 × 1107), 937 (1107 × 1110), 952 (1109 × 1110), 956 (1110), and for other possible references see index.
? Aubrey de Vere	1100 × 1105	Possibly local justiciar rather than sheriff: *RRAN*, II, no. 695; cf. nos. 576, 707.
? Alfred	probably 1112	Alfred the sheriff (county not specified) was present when land at Earls Colne, Essex, was handed over to Abingdon abbey: *Chron. Abingdon*, II, 60. Alfred may have been sheriff of Essex.
? Ralph	before 1118	*Chron. Abingdon*, II, 103; Morris, *Medieval English Sheriff*, p. 80, identifies him as Ralph Basset.
William of Buckland	1119	*Chron. Abingdon*, II, 160.

? John Belet	before 1126	Accounts for an old debt for danegeld and the penalty payments of Berkshire, responsibilities which suggest he may have been sheriff: *PR 31 Henry I*, pp. 13, 123.
Baldwin son of Clarus	before 1126	*PR 31 Henry I*, p. 122.
Anselm *vicomte* of Rouen	1127–1129	Accounts for danegeld for the third year before 1129–1130, i.e. 1127–1128: *PR 31 Henry I*, p. 124.
William de Pont de l'Arche	1129–1130	*PR 31 Henry I*, p. 124.
? Jordan de Podiis	1136 × 1154 probably late in the reign	*RRAN*, III, no. 2. His only other occurrence seems to be as witness to *RRAN*, III, no. 89 (c. 1152), issued at the siege of Newbury.
Henry of Oxford	1153, 1154–1155	*RRAN*, III, no. 13; *RBE*, II, 655–6.
? Adam the sheriff	occ. 1156	Pardoned danegeld in Berkshire: *PR 2–4 Henry II*, pp. 34, 35. Could be a retrospective reference to Stephen's reign, but probably under-sheriff, as sheriff was Richard de Camville: *PR 2–4 Henry II*, pp. 33–4. Also probably to be identified with Adam of Catmore, sheriff of the county a few years later.

Buckinghamshire

? Godric	before 1066	*DB*, I, 144b, possibly in his capacity as sheriff of Berkshire.
Ansculf de Picquigny	1066 × 1086, d. by 1086	*DB*, I, 148b.
? Ralph Taillebois	1066 × 1086	*DB*, I, 151b, sheriff of Bedfordshire.
? Hugh de Beauchamp	1087 × 1095, 1087	*RRAN*, I, no. 370 (cf. dating of 1091 × 1095 suggested in *Westminster Abbey Charters*, no. 51); II, 399. See also under **Bedfordshire** for discussion of Matthew Paris, *Chronica Majora*, VI, 34: a reference to Hugh as sheriff of Bedfordshire or Buckinghamshire.
Geoffrey	1094 × 1108	Followed Bishop Robert of Lincoln in address clause of charter of Bishop Gundulf of Rochester: *Textus Roffensis*, ff. 212r–213v, printed *Mon. Ang.*, I, 65. The charter must thus have been issued after Robert's appointment to Lincoln in 1094 and before Gundulf's death in 1108. It is tempting to identify this otherwise unknown sheriff with Geoffrey I de Mandeville, possibly sheriff of Essex, Hertfordshire and London with Middlesex.
Hugh of Buckland	1104, 1107	*RRAN*, II, nos. 676, 813.
William of Buckland	1120 × 1123	*RRAN*, II, no. 1402.
Richard	? 1125	*RRAN*, II, no. 1470, dated by editors to 1126 or 1127. However, if Maenfenin was sheriff 1125–1129, Richard must have been sheriff before that. See also *Cart. Missenden*, pt I, no. 62, pp. 63–4. This man is presumably to be identified with Richard of Winchester, sheriff of Bedfordshire.
Maenfenin	1125–1129	*PR 31 Henry I*, p. 100.
Richard Basset and Aubrey de Vere	1129–1130	*PR 31 Henry I*, p. 100.

Cambridgeshire[1]

? Orgar	before 1066	Mentioned as a landholder TRE, county not specified but probably sheriff of Cambridgeshire: *DB*, I, 197b.
Blacuin	before 1066	Described as King Edward's sheriff, county not specified but entry in account of Cambridgeshire: *DB*, I, 201b.
Aluric Godricsone	before 1086	Said in *DB* to have been entitled to a heriot from lawmen of Cambridge when he was sheriff: *DB*, I, 189.
Picot	from c. 1071	*RRAN*, I, no. 47; II, 392; (1071 × 1075), 393 (c. 1080); I, nos. 122 (1080), 129 (c. 1080, or 1081 according to *LE*, pp. 426–7); 156 (1082); *Textus Roffensis*, f. 175v: account of quarrel between Bishop Gundulf of Rochester and Picot about Freckenham, Suffolk.
	sheriff in 1086 date of death not known	*DB*, I, 199b, 200, 201b. Founded Barnwell priory with his wife. Foundation said to have been confirmed by Bishop Remigius of Lincoln shortly before the latter's death in 1092, but this chronology is not above suspicion: *Liber Memorandum de Bernewelle*, p. 44; *English Episcopal Acta*, I, no. 2, pp. 2–3.
? Roger of Huntingdon	1100 × 1102	*RRAN*, II, no. 586. Sheriff of Huntingdonshire and probably Surrey.
Gilbert [the knight]	possibly from 1107 to 1125	*RRAN*, II, nos. 939 (1109 × 1114), 1066 (concerns Cambridgeshire), 1437, 1438, 1438a, 1438b (all 1107 × 1125); for date of his death: *Records of Merton Priory*, p. 5. Sheriff also of Huntingdonshire and Surrey.
Fulk nephew of Gilbert	probably from 1125 to 1129	*Records of Merton Priory*, p. 5; *PR 31 Henry I*, p. 44. As Fulk nephew of Gilbert occurs as witness: *Cart. Ram.*, I, 139. Sheriff also of Huntingdonshire and Surrey.
Richard Basset and Aubrey de Vere	1129–1130	*PR 31 Henry I*, p. 43.
Fulk	1133 × 1160	Witnessed notifications of Abbot Walter (1133–1160): *Cart. Ram.*, I, 151–2; *Chron. Ram.*, p. 272.
? Payn (of Hemingford)	1139 × 1140	Witnesses a grant by Stephen from mills at Huntingdon issued at Cambridge: *RRAN*, III, no. 410.
	1154–1155	Accounts for Cambridge for one quarter of the year: *RBE*, II, 655.
	1155–1156	*PR 2–4 Henry II*, p. 14. Also sheriff of Huntingdonshire and Surrey.

---

1. In the early twelfth century this county was held with Huntingdonshire and Surrey: see Introduction, p. 14.

St Radegund, p. 75: witnessed a charter of Constance for St Radegund addressed to Bishop Nigel of Ely and Eustace her husband (d. 17 August 1153), for the soul of Queen Matilda (d. 3 May 1152), and for the good estate of King Stephen. It would appear that this charter was issued before Stephen's death. Possibly to be identified with Ralph, sheriff of Surrey.

Carlisle/Cumberland

It is not clear whether the following men were strictly speaking royal sheriffs. William Rufus established a base at Carlisle in 1092 and may have appointed a sheriff. The region was granted to Ranulf Meschin, probably after 1106,[1] though recovered when Ranulf became earl of Chester in 1120. Richer who is listed below may therefore have been Ranulf's sheriff rather than the king's. Hildret, who accounted for Carlisle in 1129/1130, was not described as a sheriff.

William son of Theoderic	1092 × 1100	*RRAN*, I, no. 463.
G.	1095 × 1100	*RRAN*, I, no. 478.
Richer	c. 1106 × 1112	*Mon. Ang.*, III, 583: a charter of Ranulf Meschin addressed to Richer, sheriff of Carlisle, founding Wetheral priory and granting it to St Mary's York under Abbot Stephen (d. 1112, *Heads of Religious Houses*, p. 84, and see p. 97, where c. 1106 is suggested as the foundation date of Wetheral). Richer is possibly to be identified with Richer de Boivill, for whom see Barrow, *Anglo-Norman Era*, p. 176.
Odard	before 1128	*PR 31 Henry I*, p. 142. Possibly Odard, sheriff of Northumberland or Odard de Logis, lord of Wigton, *Chron. Cumbrie*, p. 492. Hildret (see following entry) had a son Odard, but it is obviously unlikely that father succeeded son: Round, *Genealogist*, VIII (1892), 200–4.
Hildret	1128–1130 and possibly earlier	*PR 31 Henry I*, p. 142.

[handwritten marginal note:] but it would have been v. normal for a son to have been named after his grandfather

---

1. The only date establishing Ranulf's tenure of Carlisle is the foundation charter of Wetheral, see above.

Cheshire

No royal sheriffs of Cheshire have been identified for the relevant period, but from the time of Earl Ranulf I (1120–1129) the earls of Chester appointed their own sheriffs. By the late twelfth century there was a sheriff for the city as well as the county, and it is possible that the first of the men listed below was sheriff of the city. However, Ranulf the sheriff occurs in six of Earl Ranulf II's charters, in one case as a surety for the earl,[1] and as a man of some importance was presumably sheriff of the county.

? Winebald	occ. 1120 × 1129	Possibly sheriff of the city rather than the county. The house of Winebald the sheriff in the market place was mentioned in a gift to St Werburgh's Chester dating from the time of Earl Ranulf I and included in Ranulf II's charter of confirmation: *Charters of the Earls of Chester*, no. 28; cf. no. 13, Ranulf I's charter, where the same gift is recorded, but Winebald is not described as sheriff.
Ranulf	occ. 1136 × 1153 ? 1143–1153	*Charters of the Earls of Chester*, nos. 27 (1136 × 1153), 40 (c. 1150), 69 (c. 1143 × 1144), 99 (1150 × 1153), 104 (1150 × 1153), 110 (1149 × 1153, probably 1153). It is not known when Ranulf died. A man styled *Radulfus vicecomes* occurs in several early charters of Earl Ranulf II, but in no. 180 is styled *vicomte* of Avranches, cf. nos. 175, 176, 188.

1. *Charters of the Earls of Chester*, no. 110.

Cornwall

No pre-Conquest sheriffs for the county have been identified. Nigel is listed *PRO Revised List*, p. 21, on the basis of *Mon. Ang.*, VI, 989. This is a charter of Edward the Confessor for St Michael's Mount in Cornwall, and the list of signatories suggests that this Nigel was Nigel the *vicomte*, lord of Saint-Sauveur in Normandy.

? Baldwin	1086	*DB*, IV, 72, probably Baldwin sheriff of Devon.
Turstin	1086	*DB*, IV, 204b, 224, 234, 249b, 334b, 507b. Morris, *Medieval English Sheriff*, p. 45, suggested that Turstin may have been the sheriff of the count of Mortain, of whom he was an under-tenant. However, the count did not exercise complete control over Cornwall in 1086. The king had demesne land there, and would have needed a royal agent. Also, by 1096 there was evidently a royal sheriff: see next entry.
	1103 × 1106	Turstin de Cornubia and Hamelin de Cornubia occur as witnesses to a charter of William, count of Mortain, 1103 × 1106: *CDF*, p. 437. So styled, Turstin could have been Turstin the sheriff, though this does not explain the simultaneous attribution of Hamelin as de Cornubia. He is presumably to be identified with Hamelin, tenant of the count in Cornwall in 1086.
Warin	1096	*RRAN*, I, no. 378.
Richard FitzBaldwin	1114 × 1116	*RRAN*, II, no. 1131 addressed to 'William bishop of Exeter, Richard FitzBaldwin, sheriff, and others of Devon and Cornwall'. Presumably to be identified with Richard the sheriff, present with Bernard the Scribe (of Henry I) when the abbey of Mont-Saint-Michel received lands in Cornwall: PRO 31/8/140B, II, 260.
Frewin	before 1128 c. 1100	*BF*, I, 441; *PR 31 Henry I*, p. 160; Padel, *Cambridge Medieval Celtic Studies*, VIII (1984), 20–7.
Geoffrey de Furneaux	1128–1130, and possibly earlier	*PR 31 Henry I*, p. 152.
? William FitzRichard	occ. 1140	*Gesta Stephani*, p. 100, where he is described as a man who ruled the earldom of Cornwall under the king and handed it over to Reginald, son of King Henry. Reginald was created earl of Cornwall by Matilda and held the county from 1141 until his death in 1175.
Richard de Raddon	c. 1140 × 1149 c. 1146 × 1155	*Cart. Launceston*, no. 244, p. 93; *Cart. Launceston*, no. 415, p. 153.

Derbyshire

This county was probably held jointly with Nottingham-shire throughout the relevant period, because until 1256 the two counties shared a shire court.[1] As joint tenure cannot be demonstrated in every case the sheriffs are listed separately.

Harding	1066 × 1086	*RRAN*, I, no. 223.
? E[arnwig]	1093	Notification addressed to Thomas the archbishop, Robert bishop of Chester, Earl Roger, E. the sheriff, H. de Ferrers, W. Peverel and all . . . lieges . . . of Nottinghamshire and Derbyshire: *RRAN*, I, no. 337.
Richard	1100 × 1102	*RRAN*, II, no. 538 (county not specified but concerns Derbyshire). This sheriff is presumably to be identified with Richard son of Gotse: *RRAN*, II, nos. 600 (as Richard son of G., 1101 × 1102), 723 (office not specified, 1101 × 1102).
? Helgot	1105	*RRAN*, II, no. 705.
Serlo de Burg	before 1127	*PR 31 Henry I*, p. 31. His debt as past sheriff of Derbyshire and Nottinghamshire is listed with his other debts in the Yorkshire account. This suggests that his period as sheriff dated back some years; if recent, it would have been listed immediately before the arrears of Ivo de Heriz: see next entry.
Ivo de Heriz	preceded Osbert in office	*PR 31 Henry I*, p. 7, with Nottinghamshire.
Osbert Salvain	1128–1130 and possibly earlier	*PR 31 Henry I*, p. 7, with Nottinghamshire.
Robert de Perer	1154–1155	*RBE*, II, 653, with Nottinghamshire.

---

1. See above. p. 14 and references there cited.

Devon

Heche	'on the day King Edward was alive and dead', i.e. 5 Jan. 1066	*DB*, IV, 301 (Exon Domesday).
? William de Vauville	soon after 1066	Land added to a royal manor 'in the time of William de Vauville': *DB*, I, 85b; land restored to a royal manor by same: *DB*, I, 126b. Mentioned as castellan of Exeter: BL Cotton MS Vespasian A XVIII, ff. 157r–162v, and probably to be identified with William 'Gualdi', co-commander of a force sent against the sons of King Harold in 1069: OV, II, 190.
	1069	William the sheriff is amongst the witnesses of *RRAN*, I, no. 28, concerning land in Devon and Oxfordshire. Roger the sheriff who also witnesses is probably Roger d'Ivry: see **Oxfordshire**.
Baldwin	occ. between c. 1070 and 1086	*RRAN*, I, nos. 58, 59 (1070 × 1071), 125 (as sheriff of Exeter, 1080), 135 (county unspecified, 1081); *DB*, I, 100, 105b.
? William FitzBaldwin	1096, 1087 × 1097	*RRAN*, I, nos. 378, 401 (possibly spurious).
? Hugh de Port	1087 × 1100	*RRAN*, I, no. 487 (described by the editors as 'an obvious forgery').
? Geoffrey de Mandeville	occ. 1100 × 1107	*RRAN*, II, nos. 633, 649, 662, 773.
Richard FitzBaldwin	occ. 1107 × 1128	*RRAN*, II, nos. 1131 (1114 × 1116), 1493 (1123 × 1128), as Richard the sheriff 1197 (1107 × 1118), 1269 (c. 1121 × 1128), and for other possible references see index; *PR 31 Henry I*, p. 153. Baldwin the sheriff had three sons, two of whom, William and Richard, became sheriffs, but there is no evidence that the third, Robert, ever held the office. For the family, see *Complete Peerage*, IV, 308–9. The descendants of Baldwin evidently preserved a claim to the office, since Richard's sister, Adelicia, who died in 1142, is said to have held the office, as is her daughter Matilda: *Mon. Ang.*, V, 378. Adelicia's death was recorded in the Plympton annals, where she was described as daughter of Baldwin the sheriff, which led Liebermann, *Anglo-normannische Geschichtsquellen*, p. 29 n, and Morris, *Medieval English Sheriff*, p. 105, to assume this was Baldwin de Redvers, who is mentioned later in the same entry. This is the only reference to Baldwin de Redvers as sheriff, and he is not known to have had a daughter named Adelicia. Adelicia's daughter Matilda had some right to shrieval revenues: *PR 2–4 Henry II*, pp. 47, 157–9.

Geoffrey de Furneaux	1128–1130, and possibly earlier	*PR 31 Henry I*, p. 152.
Richard FitzBaldwin	1135 × 1136	*RRAN*, III, no. 500.
Richard de Redvers	1154–1155	*RBE*, II, 653.

Dorset

Alfred	before 1066	Harmer, no. 1 = S 1063; *DB*, I, 83.
Hugh	1066 × 1086	*DB*, I, 75. This is presumably Hugh son of Grip: *RRAN*, I, nos. 109, 203. Hugh had died by the time of the Domesday Survey, when his widow is found holding many of his lands: *DB Dorset*, ed. Thorn and Thorn, notes to 23, 1; 55.
Aiulf	1086, 1087 × 1094	*DB*, I, 83; *RRAN*, I, no. 204. The gift to which this document refers was made before the record. Countess Matilda was still living in 1082. The gift of Piddlehinton was made after her death, and the record after 1087 (since it refers to the memory of William the Conqueror) and before 1094 (when Roger of Montgomery died).[1]
	sheriff in the early years of Henry I's reign	*RRAN*, II, nos. 544 (1101), 573 (1102), 754 (1105 × 1116), 896 (1100 × 1108), 1018 (1107 × 1118). Aiulf had evidently died by the time of King Henry's charter for Shaftesbury abbey, 1121 × 1122: *RRAN*, II, 346–7. However, Aiulf's debt for money taken from the farm is entered on the 1130 pipe roll with no indication that he had died: *PR 31 Henry I*, p. 14.
Warin	1107 × 1122, 1122, 1128–1129	*RRAN*, II, nos. 1369, 1341. Accounts for old farm of three counties, (Dorset, Wiltshire and presumably Somerset): *PR 31 Henry I*, p. 12.
	1129–1130	With Wiltshire: *PR 31 Henry I*, p. 12. Warin the sheriff witnessed *RRAN*, II, no. 1641.
	? 1136	Warin the sheriff (county not specified) witnessed two documents, both concerning Dorset: *RRAN*, III, nos. 434, 818.
Richard de Raddon	1154–1155	*RBE*, II, 657.

---

1. Dr. David Bates kindly sent me a copy of the text and notes on this document.

Durham

No royal sheriffs have been identified for the period before 1154. From the twelfth century the names of sheriffs appointed by the bishops of Durham may be traced in episcopal *acta*. Those issued between 1071 and 1152 have been edited by H.S. Offler;[1] the references to William and Gilbert have been kindly supplied by Professor Offler in correspondence with the author.[2] In addition to a sheriff of Durham, Bishop Rannulf appointed a sheriff called Papedy for Norhamshire after building Norham castle in 1121.[3]

Osbert	occ. 1122 × 1152	Sheriff under Bishop Rannulf and again under Bishop William; may not have been sheriff under Bishop Geoffrey (1133–1140): *Durham Episcopal Charters*, nos. 17 (1122 × 1128), 20 (c. 1122 × 1127), 35 (1146), 38 (c. 1148), 39 (c. 1149), 40 (c. 1144 × 1149), 42, 45 (1144 × 1152) as sheriff.
	1148	Witnessed a chirograph: Durham, Dean and Chapter Muniments, 4. 3. Ebor. 4: Major, in *Medieval Miscellany for Doris Mary Stenton*, p. 206.
	1151	Witnessed a charter for Bishop William now surviving only in an eighteenth-century copy, Oxford, Bodleian Library, MS Top. Yorks, e. 9, ff. 115r, 117r; also mentioned *Durham Episcopal Charters*, nos. 15 (1122 × 1128), 23 (? 1127), 24, 25 (1128), 26e (c. 1123 × 1128).
William	c. 1155 × 1158	Witnessed for Bishop Hugh: Durham, Dean and Chapter Muniments, 3. 1. Pont. 18.
Gilbert	? mid-twelfth century	Gilbert *quondam vicecomes* was mentioned in a charter of Bishop Hugh, c. 1185; Durham, Dean and Chapter Muniments, Almoner's Small Cartulary, p. 223.

---

1. *Durham Episcopal Charters* (Surtees Society, CLXXIX, 1968).
2. For a list of sheriffs of Durham whose early entries briefly survey the period before 1154, see Blair *Archaeologia Aeliana*, 4th series, XXII (1944), 22–82.
3. *Durham Episcopal Charters*, pp. 90–2, 94–5, 116–17.

Essex

Leofcild	1042 × 1043	Whitelock, *Anglo-Saxon Wills*, no. 30 = S 1530; Harmer, no. 73 = S 1117, no. 74 = S 1118, and biographical notes, pp. 564–5.
Robert FitzWymarc	before 1086	*DB*, II, 98. Robert had been a staller in King Edward's reign. See Harmer, no. 84 (1052 × 1053), for a royal writ concerning land in Essex addressed to the bishop, the earl, and Robert the staller.
Sweyn son of Robert	1066 × 1075	*RRAN*, I, nos. 84–7. It is not clear when Sweyn succeeded his father. Morris, *Medieval English Sheriff*, p. 43 n. 17, cited Eyton for the dating of Robert's death or superannuation to 1071 × 1072. Eyton, (*Shropshire Archaeological and Natural History Society Publications*, II, 16), was referring to a royal charter witnessed by Suen son of Robert and calendared *RRAN*, I (1070 × 1075, ? 1073), where it is thought to be spurious.
	1070 × 1082	*RRAN*, I, no. 163.
	1066 × 1085	*RRAN*, I, no. 209.
	living 1100	*RRAN*, II, 406, 408.
? Geoffrey de Mandeville	occ. 1066 × 1086	Two spurious writs of William the Conqueror survive, one addressed to Geoffrey the sheriff (of Essex), the other to Geoffrey de Mandeville and the sheriff of Essex: *Westminster Abbey Charters*, nos. 12, 35. His grandson claimed that Geoffrey had held this office. Hugh of Buckland was in office by 1100 (see below) and Geoffrey was dead by 1103 × 1105, when *RRAN*, II, no. 661 was issued.
? Ralph Bainard	1072 × 1076	*RRAN*, I, no. 93, and see Walker, *EHR*, XXXIX (1924), 400; *DB*, II, 1b.
Ralph	1080	*RRAN*, I, no. 122. Presumably Ralph Bainard.
N.	occ. 1085 × 1117	Addressed in writ of Abbot G. of Westminster, presumably Gilbert Crispin, abbot 1085–1117, as writ is in English: *Westminster Abbey Charters*, no. 23.
Peter de Valognes	1086, and probably earlier	*DB*, II, 3; presumably P. the sheriff addressed in *RRAN*, I, no. 214 (1078 × 1085, cf. dating suggested in *Westminster Abbey Charters*, no. 26, of 1076 × 1085).
	probably sheriff under Rufus	*RRAN*, I, nos. 442 (1087 × 1100), 417 (1093 × 1100), and as P. the sheriff in no. 436.
Hugh of Buckland	occ. between 1100 and 1115	*RRAN*, II, nos. 519, 522 (1100 × 1101), 661 (1103 × 1105), 688 (1104 × 1107), 775 (1106), 862 (1102 × 1107), 863 (1100 × 1107), 1010 (1108 × 1112, as Hugh de Book), 1090 (1108 × 1115), 1105 (1100 × 1115), 1119 (1108 × 1115).

? Hugh Lyoth	1104 × 1107	*RRAN*, II, no. 861. Possibly a mistake for Hugh of Buckland. Ralph Passelewe also mentioned was probably sheriff of Suffolk.
? Alured	1100 × 1101 1100 × 1107	Follows Hugh of Buckland in the address clauses of two royal documents, so possibly co- or under-sheriff: *RRAN*, II, nos. 519, 863. Presumably to be identified with Alfred the sheriff present when Aubrey de Vere delivered Earls Colne to Abbot Faritius of Abingdon, probably in March 1112: *Chron. Abingdon*, II, 60. Mentioned as sheriff in Henry I's confirmation for Earls Colne, and in Archbishop Ralph's charter of confirmation: *Cart. Colne*, no. 2, pp. 2–3, no. 9, pp. 5–6.
? Aldwin	1108 × 1118	Follows Hugh of Buckland in the address clause of a document issued by Queen Matilda. Aldwin was her chamberlain, and may have been addressed in that capacity: *RRAN*, II, no. 1090.
Aubrey de Vere	1115 × 1122, 1121 × 1127	*RRAN*, II, nos. 1261, 1518. For other references, possibly as sheriff: nos. 1524 (1116 × 1127), 1539 (1115 × 1127), 1551 (1123 × 1129).
? Amfrid	early twelfth century	Father-in-law of William de Sackville whose lands (mainly in Essex) were later at issue in the Anstey case, *Letters of John of Salisbury*, i, no. 131. Amfrid and his county have not been identified, but note that an Anfrid *collector* occurs in 1130, *PR 31 Henry I*, p. 103.
? Haimo de Saint Clair	1127	*RRAN*, II, no. 1498. Haimo may occur here, however, as farmer of Colchester and the lands of Eudo the steward: *PR 31 Henry I*, pp. 138–9.
William of Eynesford	1128 – Easter 1130	*PR 31 Henry I*, p. 52.
Richard Basset and Aubrey de Vere	Easter–Mich 1130	*PR 31 Henry I*, p. 52.
Geoffrey de Mandeville	1141	Empress Matilda's first charter for Geoffrey, midsummer 1141: *RRAN*, III, no. 274. Stephen's second charter, Christmas 1141: *RRAN*, III, no. 276. It is not clear whether Geoffrey acted as sheriff. In no. 543 (1139 × 1141) Geoffrey seems to be addressed in an unstated official capacity. Compare with nos. 40 (1135 × 1137), 210 (addressed to Earl Geoffrey and Haimo de Saint Clair, 1140 × 1143). If Geoffrey did act as sheriff, he may have remained in office until his arrest in the autumn of 1143: *Gesta Stephani*, pp. 160–2; for a recent reappraisal of his career, see Prestwich and Davis, *EHR*, CIII (1988), 283–317.
<Andrew Bucca Lincta	c. 1144 × 1147	*PRO Revised List*, p. 43, without source. This is presumably Andrew Buccuinte, justiciar of London in Stephen's reign: Reynolds, p. 354.>
Maurice [de Tiretot]	occ. between 1143 and 1152	*RRAN*, III, nos. 546–8 (in 548, MS reads Martin for Maurice). Also occurs in nos. 544 (c. 1143 × 1147), 552 (1143 × 1154), which concern Essex.

Richard de Luci 1154–1155 *RBE*, II, 650. Richard had previously been justiciar in this county: *RRAN*, III, no. 559 (1143 × 1147), cf. nos. 544–50, 552.

Gloucestershire

Aluui (Aelfwig)	before 1066	*DB*, I, 162b. Not specifically said to be sheriff of this county, and possibly to be identified with Alwi, sheriff of Oxfordshire.
Aluuin (Aethelwine)	died before 1066	*DB*, I, 167b. Not specifically said to be sheriff of this county. For a man of the same name, see **Hereford**, **Huntingdonshire** and **Warwickshire**.
? Brictric	? 1067	*RRAN*, I, no. 9.
Roger de Pîtres	after 1066, d. by 1086	Roger the sheriff, father of Walter, received land from Earl William (FitzOsbern): *DB*, I, 169. See also above under **Berkshire**.
Durand	1079 × 1083, 1086 d. by 1095	*RRAN*, I, no. 186; *DB*, I, 162; Round, *Feudal England*, pp. 241–5.
Walter of Gloucester	c. 1093 – c. 1126	*RRAN*, I, nos. 400 (1093 × 1097), 411 (1094 × 1098), 389 (1097) = *LE*, pp. 207–8 (1096 × 1098, prob. 1097); II, nos. 554 (1101), 629 (1100 × 1128), 678 (1104 ?), 701 (1101 × 1105), 706 (1105 × 1106), 718 (1102, 1103, 1105), 719 (1100 × 1105), 784 (1105 × 1106), 893 (1107 × 1111), 940 (1109 × 1113), 1006–9 (1100 × 1112), 1103 (1115 ?), 1266 (1115 × 1127), 1567 (1100 × 1128), and for other possible references, see index; *Cart. Worc.*, no. 24, witnesses a royal writ dated 1100 × 1130 (not in *RRAN*). For date of his retirement see: Walker, *Transactions of the Bristol and Gloucestershire Archaeological Society*, LXXVII (1958), 68.
Richard the chaplain	occ. between 1113 and 1155	Described as sheriff: *Cart. Glouc.*, I, 164. Presumably to be identified with Richard the sheriff, who attests charters of 1136 and 1138, in a Llanthony cartulary: PRO, C 115/K1/6679, ff. 21, 22; also a charter of 1148 × 1155: *Charters of the Earldom of Hereford*, no. 39. Although described as sheriff, Richard was probably the deputy in turn of Walter and then Walter's son and grandsons: see below. From 1122 there was an earl of this county.
Miles of Gloucester	c. 1126–1143 1128–1130	Son and successor of Walter: *PR 31 Henry I*, p. 76. Created earl of Hereford 1141. His elevation did not affect his position in the county.
? Roger, earl of Hereford	1143–1155	No evidence that he held the family shrievalty, and Richard the chaplain may have become the earl of Gloucester's deputy after 1143.
Walter, earl of Hereford	before Mich 1155	Accounts for old farm at Mich 1156: *PR 2–4 Henry II*, p. 48.
Osbert of Westbury	Jan–Mich 1155	*RBE*, II, 650.

Alan   occ. 1156   Probably under-sheriff 1155–1156 as Earl Walter accounted for farm in that year: *PR 2–4 Henry II*, p. 50.

Hampshire

Eadsige	c. 1053 1066 and earlier	*ASChs.*, no. 114 = S 1476. Presumably to be identified with 'Ezi the sheriff' who occurs as a landholder both TRE and after King Edward's death but before the coming of King William: *DB*, I, 43, 48b.
? Ralph de Limesi	1066 × 1086	Occurs in *DB* as having 'received' a royal manor, a term which suggests he held the manor as farmer, and possibly as sheriff: *DB*, I, 39.
? Hugh de Port	1070 × 1087, 1086 × 1087	Addressed in royal documents, possibly as sheriff: *RRAN*, I, nos. 267, 284; II, 398. In 1086 he was the most important lay landholder in Hampshire and in 1096 was described as *vicarius* of Winchester at the time when he became a monk at St Peter's Gloucester: *RRAN*, I, no. 379. Presumably to be identified with Hugh the sheriff: *RRAN*, I, no. 270; *DB*, I, no. 47. Round pointed out that this identification is not beyond question because Hugh the sheriff, his wife Hadewisa, and son Simon occur in the *Liber Vitae* of the Old Minster at Winchester: *VCH Hampshire*, I, 423–4. Yet this Hugh the sheriff need not have been sheriff of Hampshire. The wife of Hugh son of Grip, sheriff of Dorset, was named Hadewise, for instance. See under **Dorset**.
Durand	1096, 1096 × 1100	*RRAN*, I, no. 377; II, 403, 407–8.
Henry de Port	1101 × 1103, 1103 × 1105	*RRAN*, II, nos. 638, 687, and for other possible references see index.
William de Pont de l'Arche	1110, 1127 1128–1130 possibly continuously until his death c. 1148	As sheriff of Southampton: *RRAN*, II, nos. 947, 948; concerning land near Southampton: *RRAN*, II, nos. 1507, 1508; *PR 31 Henry I*, p. 36. William was chamberlain in charge of the treasury at Winchester in 1135, when he was persuaded to hand the keys to King Stephen. He was still in the city, apparently in the royal castle, in 1141. His latest attestation for the Empress can be dated between 1144 and 1147: *Gesta Stephani*, pp. 9, 150–2; *RRAN*, III, no. 277; Mason, *Bulletin of the Institute of Historical Research*, LIII (1980), 3 and n. 30.

Herefordshire

Bruning	1016 × 1035	*ASChs.*, no. 78 = S 1462.
Leofric	1017 × 1030	Harmer, no. 48 = S 991, cf. *ASChs.*, nos. 81 = S 1423, 83 = S 1460.
Ulfceteles	1043 × 1046	*ASChs.*, no. 99 = S 1469.
Aelfnoth	1056	*ASC s.a.* 1056.
? Osbern	1061 × 1066	Harmer, no. 50 (office not specified, but could have been sheriff).
? A¹uuin	before 1086	Mentioned as a landholder TRE in Herefordshire but not necessarily sheriff of this county: *DB*, I, 185. For a man of the same name see **Gloucestershire**, **Huntingdonshire** and **Warwickshire**.
John	before 1086	Mentioned as a landholder TRE in Herefordshire but was not necessarily sheriff of this county: *DB*, I, 184.
Ralf de Bernai	1066 × 1086	*DB*, I, 181; *Hemingi Chartularium*, I, 250. Possibly under the authority of William FitzOsbern: Lewis, *Anglo-Norman Studies*, VII (1985), 207–8.
? Ilbert	occ. 1086	*DB*, I, 179b: holds Archenfield at farm from the king. Possibly to be identified with Ilbert FitzTurold.
? Gilbert	occ. 1086	*DB*, I, 183: holds Clifford at farm. Probably to be identified with Gilbert FitzTurold: Lewis, *Anglo-Norman Studies*, VII (1985), 207.
? Hugh de Lacy	1100	*RRAN*, II, no. 500.
? Adam de Port	1107 × 1115 1100 × 1128 1121	*RRAN*, II, nos. 990, 1101, 1385, 1243, 1265; died 1130 × 1133: *Herefordshire Domesday*, p. 128.
? Payn FitzJohn	1123 × 1127 c. 1135 c. 1136 d. 1137	*RRAN*, II, no. 1392; Writ of Henry I addressed to Payn FitzJohn and his ministers of Shropshire and Herefordshire: *Cart. Worc.*, no. 153 (not in *RRAN*); *RRAN*, III, no. 382, and see no. 398. JW, p. 43.
? Humphrey	1132	Humphrey the sheriff (county not specified) is mentioned in a notification by Robert, bishop of Hereford, of decision in a lawsuit: Oxford, Balliol College MS 271, f. 88r. Possibly reeve of Droitwich: see under **Worcestershire**.

? Miles of Gloucester	c. 1136, 1141	*RRAN*, III, nos. 382, 701.
Maurice	1148 × 1155, 1148 × 1160 c. 1150 × 1155 1154–1155	*Charters of the Earldom of Hereford*, nos. 17, 18, 33; *Letters and Charters of Gilbert Foliot*, nos. 302, 305; BL Addit. Ch. 19588; *RBE*, II, 650; attested charter of Hugh of Kilpeck for Reading: *Reading Abbey Cartularies*, I, no. 327, pp. 263–4.
Walter, earl of Hereford	before Jan 1155	*PR 2–4 Henry II*, p. 50.

Hertfordshire

Edmund	? 1067	*RRAN*, I, no. 16.
Ilbert of Hertford	1066 × 1087, 1072 × 1075 before 1086	*RRAN*, I, no. 250; II, 391; Round, *Feudal England*, pp. 349–50. *DB*, I, 132b, 133, 142.
Ralph Taillebois	before 1086	*DB*, I, 133; living 1075: *LE*, p. 196. Evidently dead by 1086. Sheriff of Bedfordshire and probably Buckinghamshire.
Peter de Valognes	1086 and possibly earlier ? 1087 × 1089, 1087 × 1092	*DB*, I, 132b, 133, 135b; for possible references to Peter as sheriff: *RRAN*, I, nos. 93 (1070 × 1076), 235 (1080 × 1086), 277 (1085 × 1087). *RRAN*, II, 399, 400.
? Geoffrey de Mandeville	before c. 1100	*RRAN*, III, no. 275, and see **Essex**.
H.	1087 × 1093	*RRAN*, I, no. 346. Probably Hugh of Buckland.
Hugh of Buckland	1100, 1100 × 1108, 1105	*RRAN*, II, nos. 488, 620, 684, and for other possible references see index.
William of Eynesford	1128–Easter 1130	*PR 31 Henry I*, p. 52.
Richard Basset and Aubrey de Vere	Easter–Mich 1130	*PR 31 Henry I*, p. 52.
Geoffrey de Mandeville	1141	*RRAN*, III, no. 276, and see notes under **Essex**.
Guy son of Tyece, and Henry of Essex	1154–1155, each for half of the year	*RBE*, II, 651.

Huntingdonshire

? Aluuin — before 1086 — *DB*, I, 206b, where he occurs as a landholder TRE. Not necessarily sheriff of Huntingdonshire. For a man of the same name see **Gloucestershire**, **Herefordshire** and **Warwickshire**.

Aluric — before 1066, and possibly after — Harmer, no. 59 = S 1107; Aluric is said to have had a messuage TRE which King William granted to his wife and sons: *DB*, I, 203; cf. 208b, where he is said to have paid the farm of Keyston (a royal manor), and his sons after him, until Eustace took the shrievalty. Aluric is presumably to be identified with Aluric son of Godric: see under **Cambridgeshire**.

Eustace — 1080, 1086 — *RRAN*, I, no. 122; *DB*, I, 206, 208.

Roger — ? c. 1080 — Witnessed agreement between Odo the steward and Ailsi abbot of Ramsey; other witnesses include Rannulf brother of Ilger: *Cart. Ram.*, I, 232–3.

G. son of Roger — 1087 × 1100 — Addressed in writ of William Rufus: *Chron. Ram.*, p. 210.

Rannulf brother of Ilger — occ. between 1092 and 1100 — *RRAN*, I, nos. 329 (1092, as Ranulf), 413 (1087 × 1093, address should read Ranulf brother of Ilger, no office specified), 477 (1094 × 1100, address should read Ranulf, no office specified).

Roger of Huntingdon — 1100 × 1102, 1100 × 1110, 1103 — *RRAN*, II, nos, 528A, 574, 650, and see also nos. 581–2.

Gilbert the knight — occ. between 1106 and 1125 — *RRAN*, II, nos. 966–7 (1107 × 1111), 1262a (1121, county not specified but concerns Huntingdonshire), 1414 (1110 × 1123), 1438 (1107 × 1125), 1438a (1106 × 1125), 1438b (1107 × 1125), and for other possible references see index; mentioned (county not specified but concerns Huntingdonshire, 1110): *Chron. Ram.*, p. 365; heard dispute between abbots of Thorney and Peterborough, 1114 × 1125: CUL Addit. MS 3021, f. 419r. For date of death: *Records of Merton Priory*, p. 5.

Fulk nephew of Gilbert — probably 1125–1129 — *RRAN*, II, nos. 1452, 1456, 1462 (county not specified but concerns Huntingdonshire); *Cart. Ram.*, I, 144 (1127); CUL Addit. MS 3020, f. 145r (1127); CUL Addit. MS 3021, f. 317v, printed Stenton, *English Justice*, pp. 143, 145.

Richard Basset and Aubrey de Vere — 1129–1130 — *PR 31 Henry I*, p. 43.

? William of Eynesford — 1100 × 1133 — *RRAN*, II, no. 1837.

Fulk	1133 × 1160	*Cart. Ram.*, I, 152; *Chron. Ram.*, p. 272 (county not specified but concerns Huntingdonshire).
Payn [of Hemingford]	1139 × 1148	Saltman, *Theobald, Archbishop of Canterbury*, no. 301 (as Payn),
	1150 × 1161	no. 302, pp. 528–9.
	? 1148 × 1153	*English Episcopal Acta*, I, no. 267.
	Easter–Mich 1155	*RBE*, II, 653. See also *RRAN*, III, no. 410 (1139 × 1140), possibly as sheriff of Cambridgeshire. Payn was also sheriff of Cambridgeshire and Surrey.
? Robert Grimbald	before 1155	*PRO Revised List*, p. 66, without source. Robert was sheriff of Northamptonshire, 1154–1155, and 1136 × 53 (see p. 64).

Kent

Wulfsige	964 × 988	*Charters of Rochester*, no. 34 = S 1458.
Leofric	995 × 1006	*Charters of Rochester*, no. 69 = S 1456.
Aethelwine	c. 1016 × 1020	*ASChs.*, no. 77 = S 1461; Harmer, no. 26 = S 985.
Osweard	before 1066	Harmer, no. 35 = S 1090, no. 39 = S 1092; *DB*, I, 2b.
? Aethelnoth	c. 1066	'Aethelnoth, governor of Canterbury (*satrapa Cantwariensis*)' was one of those taken back to Normandy by King William in 1067: FW *s.a.* 1067.
? Hugh de Port	c. 1066 × 1070	His predecessor in some of his Kentish estates was Osweard, probably Osweard the sheriff: *DB*, I, 8a, 9b, 10b, 2c.
Haimo *dapifer*	occurs from 1077, in office 1086 and later, died before 1100	*RRAN*, I, nos. 98–100 (1077), 101 (1077?), 175–6 (1070 × 1082), 328 (1092), 355 (1087 × 1094), 435 (1085 × 1100), 458 (1089 × 1100) and also witnesses no. 450. In other documents he is addressed simply as Haimo *dapifer* (nos. 102, 304, 340, 372). No. 260 is also addressed to Haimo the sheriff and H. *dapifer* whom the editor suggested was Haimo *dapifer*. For references to Haimo *dapifer* see *DB*, I, 2, 3b, 4, 6, 6b, 7, 9b; *Domesday Monachorum*, pp. 55–6; Haimo was evidently dead by the time *RRAN*, I, no. 451 was issued. Because of the difficulty of establishing when Haimo I died, some of the later references above may actually refer to his son and successor, Haimo II.
Haimo II *dapifer*	succeeded father and held office until 1114	*RRAN*, II, no. 634 (1101 × 1103), 635 (1100 × 1103), 647 (1100 × 1103), 845 (1107, county not specified but concerns Kent), 1081 (1108 × 1114, county not specified but concerns Kent). In other documents he is addressed simply as Haimo *dapifer* (nos. 516, 517, 570, 670, 872, 873, 878, 901, 934, 943, 1021, 1077, 1135, 1140, 1141, 1142, 1157, 1161). See also nos. 652, 868, each addressed to Haimo the sheriff and witnessed by Haimo *dapifer*. These could be taken as implying that there were two men, but the form of address may simply have reflected Haimo's official capacity in the county.
William of Eynesford	1114 × 1116, 1116 × 1118, 1124 × 1129, 1127	*RRAN*, II, nos. 1093, 1189, 1191–2, 1497, 1511.
Rualon	1129–1130	*PR 31 Henry I*, p. 63. Almost certainly Rualon d'Avranches who occurs on p. 65.

Ansfrid	1131 × 1133	*RRAN*, II, no. 1728. It is very difficult to distinguish Ansfrid the sheriff from other men named Ansfrid who occur in documents relating to Kent. Both Haimo the steward and the archbishop of Canterbury seem to have had stewards named Ansfrid: see *RRAN*, II, nos. 845 and 1867. It is tempting to identify all three as one man, but the situation is complicated by references to Ansfrid the clerk; see, for example, *RRAN*, II, no. 1728, and compare with no. 845, where Ansfrid the clerk and Ansfrid, steward of Haimo, both appear.
William	1130 × 1133	*RRAN*, II, no. 1867. Presumably William of Eynesford.
Ansfrid	1136	*RRAN*, III, no. 142.
Ralph Picot	occurs in documents dated between 1143 and 1161; sheriff by 1148	Saltman, *Theobald, Archbishop of Canterbury*, no. 55 (1143 × 1148) p. 281, no. 225 (1150 × 1161) p. 453, and see also pp. 536 (1155), 542 (1149 × 1154).
	in office 1153	Christ Church Canterbury Register A, see *HMC 8th Report*, pt I, App., p. 329.
	1155, Jan–Mich	*RBE*, II, 648.
? William of Ypres	before Christmas 1154	William was very powerful in Kent in 1154 and took precedence over Ralph Picot in the address clause of *RRAN*, III, no. 165. *Chron. Battle*, pp. 144–5, states that William held the county; see also Gervase of Canterbury, *Historical Works*, II, 73. There is no evidence, however, that he was ever sheriff.

Lancashire

No sheriffs have been identified for the pre-Conquest period. After the Conquest Roger of Poitou, third son of Roger of Montgomery, received a large estate in Lancashire, but seems to have lost it shortly before 1086. Initially he joined the rebellion against Rufus in 1088 but then changed sides, subsequently recovering his estates in England. His lands in Lancashire were enlarged to encompass the whole of the county, and are thought to have been confiscated when the family of Montgomery-Bellême was expelled from England in 1102.[1] The honour was conferred on Stephen of Blois before 1124 – probably between 1113 and 1118.[2] King David of Scotland took over the north of the county by 1141.[3] Stephen granted both the honour of Lancaster (north Lancashire), and the land 'between Ribble and Mersey', to Earl Ranulf II of Chester in 1146.[4] A charter issued by Ranulf for the land 'between the Ribble and the Mersey' (i.e. south Lancashire), was addressed to his justices there.[5] David ceded the honour of Lancaster to Ranulf in 1149,[6] and Prince Henry confirmed Ranulf in possession of both parts of the county in 1153.[7] Ranulf died in the same year, and both regions passed to King Stephen's son William.

Godfrey	1094

CDF, no. 665: charter of the lord of Lancaster witnessed by Godfrey who was evidently his sheriff.

1. This account is based on Barlow, *William Rufus*, pp. 91, 333. For Roger of Montgomery and his family: Mason, *Transactions of the Royal Historical Society*, 5th series, XIII (1963), 1–28.
2. The *terminus ad quem* for Stephen's acquisition of Lancaster is his foundation of Furness in 1124, though he may have acquired the honour earlier, as he was in possession of the Lincolnshire lands of Roger of Poitou by 1118 as the Lindsey Survey shows: *The Lincolnshire Domesday and the Lindsey Survey, passim*.
3. Differing views have been expressed about the history of the county under Stephen, based on charters issued by Stephen, David, and Earl Ranulf. See Farrer in *VCH Lancashire*, I, 293–5; Tait, *Mediaeval Manchester and the Beginnings of Lancashire*, pp. 165–74. Cronne, *EHR*, L (1935), 670–80 argued that David acquired the north of the county in 1144 and the south after the arrest of the earl of Chester in 1146. Yet David was in possession of northern Lancashire by 1141, if not several years earlier: Barrow, *EHR*, LXX (1955), 85–9; the evidence was discussed by Green in a conference paper delivered at Chester in July 1988, to be published by the *Chester Archaeological Society*.
4. *RRAN*, III, no. 178.
5. *Shrewsbury Cart.*, II, 313.
6. John of Hexham, *Historia*, in SD, II, 323.
7. *RRAN*, III, no. 180.

Leicestershire

? Hugh de Grandmesnil	before 1093	Explicit evidence of tenure is lacking, but it is hard to identify anyone else who could have been sheriff at this date. OV, II, 265, says that Hugh received the *municipatum* of Leicester. Hugh died in 1093: OV, IV, 336–7.
? Ivo de Grandmesnil	1093 × 1102	OV, VI, 18–20.
Robert de Pavilli	1101 × 1108 1102 × 1106	*Magnum Registrum Album*, no. 687; *RRAN*, II, no. 793.
Hugh of Leicester	by 1108	Attests William Peverel's foundation charter of Lenton priory. Other witnesses include Gerard, archbishop of York (d. 1108): *Mon. Ang.*, V, 111.
	before 1129	*PR 31 Henry I*, p. 81. Occurs in documents not dealing with this county as Hugh of Leicester, e.g. *RRAN*, II, nos. 1156 (1107 × 1116), 1317, 1318 (1122). It seems unlikely that he lost the county before Mich 1129.
Hugh de Warelville	Mich 1129–Easter 1130	*PR 31 Henry I*, p. 85.
Richard Basset and Aubrey de Vere	Easter–Mich 1130	*PR 31 Henry I*, p. 81.
? Ralph	1139 × 1147	*Reg. Antiq.*, II, no. 324, possibly as sheriff of Lincolnshire. If he was sheriff of Leicestershire he may have been Ralph the butler, steward of the earl of Leicester, who retired in 1140. For Ralph see Crouch, *Beaumont Twins, passim*.
Geoffrey l'Abbé	1154–1155	*RBE*, II, 655. Geoffrey was son of Ralph (above) and the earl's steward also.

Lincolnshire[1]

Merlosuein	1066	Landholder TRE whose lands had passed to Ralph Paynel by 1086: *DB*, I, 376b;
	1067	*RRAN*, I, no. 8. Rebelled 1069, *ASC*.
Turold	1066 × 1086	*DB*, I, 346b; *RRAN*, I, no. 430 (1066 × 1100 as T. the sheriff); II, 398, no. 288d (1070 × 1087). Turold may have been established in England before 1066 and was related to Lucy, who married Ivo Taillebois: Green, *Anglo-Norman Studies*, V (1983), p. 132n.
<Earnwig	1075 × 1092	*RRAN*, II, no. 333 is addressed to Thomas, archbishop of York, and Turold and Earnwig his sheriff (or sheriffs ?) and all his thanes in Nottinghamshire and Lincolnshire;
	1091 × 1092	no. 335 is similarly addressed. The order suggests that Earnwig was sheriff of Lincolnshire and Turold of Nottinghamshire but the order of the counties appears to have been inverted.>
H.	1076 × 1085	*RRAN*, I, no. 212. Possibly to be identified with Hugh de Port, sheriff of Nottinghamshire. Another possibility is Hugh son of Baldric, sheriff of Yorkshire.
? Norman Crassus	before Ivo	*DB*, I, 376.
Ivo Taillebois	1086	*DB*, I, 376, cf. *RRAN*, I, no. 406. First husband of Lucy: *Complete Peerage*, VII, App. J.
N.	1087 × 1088	*RRAN*, I, no. 305. Possibly to be identified with Norman Crassus.
Osbert	occ. between 1093 and 1116	*RRAN*, I, nos. 374 (1093 × 1095), 407, 408 (1093 × 1098), 409 (1095 × 1097), 467, 469, 470 (1093 × 1100), 479 (1095 × 1100) = B & C, no. 29 (1095); II, nos. 504 (1100), 531, 534–8 (1101), 571 (1102), 587 (1100 × 1107), 588 (1101 × 1107), 642 (1103 × 1106), 727 (1100 × 1115), 746, 772, 781 (1103 × 1106), 795 (1106 ?), 821 (1100 × 1107), 844 (1107), 888 (1100 × 1108), 889 (1100 × 1115), 964, 965 (1106 × 1115), 968 (1100 × 1116), 1115, 1116, 1118, 1120 (1100 × 1115). There is no indication that

1.   The following list owes much to that by Farrer, *EHR*,
     XXX (1902), 277–85.

Osbert's tenure was interrupted, so R[anulf] FitzRanulf who occurs in no. 818 (1102 × 1107) may have been local justiciar. Ranulf may have been Ranulf Meschin, third husband of Lucy: see above. Osbert's successor in office was probably Wigod but *PRO Revised List*, p. 78, suggests Walter de Gant, without citing a source. *RRAN*, II, no. 1097 (1115 × 1116), is addressed to Robert bishop of Lincoln, Walter de Gant and all the barons of Lincolnshire. However this is a notification of the elevation of Bardney into an abbey at the prayer of Walter de Gant, so Walter was not necessarily being addressed in any capacity other than founder.

Wigod of Lincoln	1114 × 1116, 1115 × 1122	*RRAN*, II, nos. 1138, 1374.
Hugh of Leicester	1120 × 1122	*RRAN*, II, no. 1254; *PR 31 Henry I*, p. 81.
? William Torniant	before 1128	*PR 31 Henry I*, p. 109. This debt may, however, have been incurred by William's father, Osbert: see above.
Rayner of Bath	1128–1130	*PR 31 Henry I*, p. 109; *RRAN*, II, nos. 1640, 1652.
William son of Hacon	1133	*RRAN*, II, no. 1784. Apparently still living 1149 × 1150 when witnesses a charter of Gilbert de Gant: BL Addit. MS 40008, f. 320.
Hugh son of Eudo	1135 × 1139	*Reg. Antiq.*, VII, no. 2050.
? Ralph	1139 × 1147	*Reg. Antiq.*, II, no. 324, possibly as sheriff of Leicestershire.
Jordan de Blosseville	1154–1155	*RBE*, II, 656.

London and Middlesex

It is not easy to distinguish sheriffs of Middlesex from others named in material relating to Middlesex or to London. Reeves of London, stallers, and justices all occur at various dates, and on occasion the king might also address his instructions to moneyers, to his chamberlain of London, or to his castellans. The list which follows here has thus to take account of an unusually wide range of possibilities. Particular attention is drawn to the relationship between the offices of reeve of London and sheriff of Middlesex, for this county was unique in being a small county dominated by its principal city. Even before 1066 it is possible that one of the reeves of London was also sheriff of Middlesex. This situation recurred shortly after the Conquest and had evidently become customary by 1128 as the 1130 pipe roll reveals, though there is insufficient evidence to establish precisely when the two offices were united. For a detailed discussion of these problems see Reynolds, *History*, LVII (1972), 337–57; Brooke and Keir, *London*, pp. 191–218, 371–4.

Ulf	occ. 1044 × 1051, prob. 1044 × 1046	Harmer, no. 77 = S 1121. Presumably Ulf the portreeve: Harmer, no. 75 (1042 × 1044) = S 1119. Possibly also Wulfgar the portreeve: Harmer, no. 51 (1042 × 1044) = S 1103, as suggested by Brooke and Keir, p. 371. This presumably explains why they suggested dates of 1042–1044 for Ulf as sheriff. See also Brooke and Keir, *London*, p. 193 and Harmer, pp. 50,52.
Aelfgaet	occ. 1051 × 1066, prob. 1057 × 1066	Harmer, nos. 86 = S 1130, 87 = S 1131.
Gosfregth	occ. 1070 × 1087	*RRAN*, I, no. 265. Possibly to be identified with Gosfregth the portreeve of London addressed in a writ of William I, c. 1067: *RRAN*, I, no. 15 = B & C, no. 15. Both may in turn be identified with Geoffrey de Mandeville: see next entry.
? Geoffrey de Mandeville	1087 × 1100	*RRAN*, I, no. 444, cf. nos. 278, 306; see also III, no. 275, for the claim allowed by King Stephen that this office had been held by Geoffrey I de Mandeville.
? Ralph Bainard	1075 × 1085	*RRAN*, I, no. 211, possibly as castellan of Baynard's castle.
Roger	1086	*DB*, I, 127, 129b. Perhaps to be identified with Roger de Raimes, the only tenant-in-chief in this county named Roger, other than Earl Roger of Montgomery.
? Richard del Parc	1087 × 1100	*RRAN*, I, no. 444; II, 406–7; Geoffrey de Mandeville precedes Richard in the address clause.
? Ralph de Marci and Wolfric of Holborn	1093 × 1097	*RRAN*, II, no. 404.
? William Bainard	1100	*RRAN*, II, no. 532, possibly as castellan of Baynard's castle. Preceded in the address clause by Hugh of Buckland, probably sheriff from 1100: see below.
? Roger de Valognes	occ. 1100 × 1107, poss. 1100 × 1101	*RRAN*, II, no. 556.

Hugh of Buckland	1100 × 1104	BL Cotton MS Otho D III, f. 73r: a charter of William, count of Mortain, addressed to Hugh of Buckland the sheriff and all the liege men of King Henry, French and English, of Middlesex.[1] King Henry's charter of confirmation is calendared (from a defective copy which does not mention Hugh) in *RRAN*, II, no. 741 (dated 1105 × 1106).
	1108	*Cart. Aldgate*, no. 1072.
	? 1100 − ? 1115	The two references noted above alone state explicitly that Hugh was sheriff, but there are others which indicate that Hugh was in authority from 1100 until his death in 1115 or 1116: see under **Bedfordshire**. *RRAN*, II, nos. 532 (1100), 543 (1100 × 1107), 646 (1102 × 1103), 666 (1103 × 1104), 702 (1101 × 1107), 769 (1100 × 1106), 898 (1107 × 1115), 972, 980 (1108 × 1111), 982 (1111), 991 (1111), 1105 (1100 × 1115), 1123 (1107 × 1115), and 730* (1103 × 1105). Reynolds, *History*, LVII (1972), 354 and Brooke and Keir, *London*, p. 372, suggest he may have been a justice rather than a sheriff, but without supporting evidence.
? Roger	1107 × 1115	*RRAN*, II, no. 898; *Chron. Ram.*, p. 237. Possibly Roger de Valognes, or Roger nephew of Hubert.
? Otto the goldsmith	1107 × 1115	*RRAN*, II, no. 898.
? Leofstan	1107 × 1115	*RRAN*, II, no. 898. Described as reeve of London: *Cart. Aldgate*, no. 1072. Listed by Reynolds, *History*, LVII (1972), 354, and Brooke and Keir, *London*, p. 372, as a possible sheriff, but only a candidate if Hugh of Buckland was justice.
? Rainer	1111	*RRAN*, II, no. 982, addressed to Hugh of Buckland and Rainer the reeve. Listed by Reynolds, *History*, LVII (1972), 354, and Brooke and Keir, *London*, p. 372, as a possible sheriff, but as in the preceding case he is only a candidate if Hugh of Buckland was justice. Reynolds also draws attention to the possibility that Rainer was the reeve of Abingdon abbey.
? William the chamberlain	1107 × 1115	*RRAN*, II, no. 898, possibly as chamberlain of London, cf. no. 1377, and *PR 31 Henry I*, p. 145. For the office see Kellaway, *Studies in London History*, pp. 75–91, at pp. 76–7.
<? Gilbert Prutfort	before 1115	*PRO Revised List*, p. 199, without source: presumably a reference to the man of this name who was sheriff in Stephen's reign.>
William of Eynesford	1114 × 1130	*Cart. Ram.*, I, 139, where an under-sheriff named John is mentioned. Possibly John son of Ralph FitzEbrard, who occurs in 1130: see below.

---

1.   This reference was kindly supplied by Dr. D. Bates.

Aubrey de Vere with Roger nephew of Hubert	1120 × 1122 1125	*RRAN*, II, no. 1315, cf. nos. 1377, 1487. Round, *Geoffrey de Mandeville*, p. 309.
Ralph FitzEbrard	before 1128	In 1130 Ralph's son John accounted for his father's arrears of the farm: *PR 31 Henry I*, p. 144.
Fulk FitzWalter	1128–1129	*PR 31 Henry I*, p. 144, cf. *RRAN*, II, no. 1610a, addressed to Fulk FitzWalter and Eustace the sheriff and all the barons of London. Unless this writ was issued before 1128 (the editors suggest 1129) Eustace must have been under-sheriff.
William Lelutre, Geoffrey Bucherell, Ralph FitzHerlewin, William de Balio	1129–1130	*PR 31 Henry I*, p. 149.
Osbert Huitdeniers	1136 × 1143	Thomas Becket was a clerk in the household of his kinsman Osbert according to FitzStephen: *Materials for the History of Thomas Becket*, III, 14. Edward Grim states that Becket was clerk to a sheriff, without naming Osbert: *Materials for the History of Thomas Becket*, II, 363; Brooke and Keir, *London*, p. 212 n.3 and references there cited.
N.	1138 × 1157, prob. before 1154	Addressed as sheriff of Middlesex in writ of Abbot G. of Westminster: *Westminster Abbey Charters*, no. 274 (editor suggests that this was Gervase, abbot 1138–1157, and that the writ almost certainly dates from Stephen's reign, as there is no known N. the sheriff for the early years of Henry II).
Gilbert Becket	before c. 1139	*Materials for the History of Thomas Becket*, III, 14; Brooke and Keir, *London*, p. 212, suggest soon after 1130.
Ranulf	1139 × 1158 ? before 1154	BL Addit. Ch. 65175: a charter of Earl Robert de Ferrers attested by Ranulf, sheriff of London. The limits of dating are those of Robert's tenure of the earldom of Derby, but Ranulf was presumably in office before 1154, as no sheriff of this name is known thereafter. Ranulf is possibly to be identified with Ranulf the sheriff who occurs as a witness in a mid-twelfth century charter issued by a member of a prominent London family: *Cart. Colchester*, II, 294; Brooke and Keir, *London*, p. 373 (mid-twelfth century).
Gilbert Prutfot (Proudfoot)	1138 × 1142, ? 1143	*HMC 9th Report*, App. p. 62; *Mon. Ang.*, III, 310; Brooke and Keir, *London*, pp. 213–14.
Geoffrey de Mandeville	1141	*RRAN*, III, no. 276, and see notes under **Essex**.
John	1141	*RRAN*, III, no. 530 ? to be identified with John FitzRalf, see below.
<? Maurice	1151	*PRO Revised List*, p. 199, without source. This was perhaps Maurice sheriff of Essex.>

<? Brithstan	c. 1153	*PRO Revised List*, p. 199, without source. Entry probably based on notification of Abbot Laurence of Westminster to Brithstan, sheriff of Middlesex: BL Cotton MS Faustina A III, ff. 258b–259. However, Laurence did not become abbot until c. 1157, and this reference is probably to Brihtmar of Haverhill, one of the sheriffs of London between 1157 and 1159: Reynolds, *History*, LVII (1972), 355.>
John FitzRalf	Oct 1154–Easter 1155	Accounted for the farm of London *de termino quo Rex Stephanus mortuus fuit usque ad pascha proxime sequens*: *PR 7 Henry II*, p. 17. Stephen died 25 Oct 1154. Possibly John son of Ralf FitzEbrard, see above.
	Christmas 1155–1157	with Gervase of Cornhill, *PR 2–4 Henry II*, p. 3.
Gregory	half of the year 1154–1155	*RBE*, II, 658; sheriffs at Michaelmas 1156 account for pleas and murder fines 'of the time of Gregory': *PR 2–4 Henry II*, pp. 5, 115.

Norfolk

Norfolk was often, though not invariably, held jointly with Suffolk, and comparison should be made with the list for that county. Of earlier lists of sheriffs of the county, see especially Round, *EHR*, XXXV (1920), 481–96; Landon, *Norfolk Archaeology*, XXIII (1929), 147–64.

? Ailwy	1040 × 1042	Addressed (office not specified but document concerns Thetford) in writ of Harthacnut: Harmer, no. 56 = S 996. Probably Ailwy of Thetford: see below.
Toli	before 1066	Harmer, no. 61 = S 1109. Writ is not authentic, but address clause may have been taken from an authentic document. Mentioned *DB*, II, 211b, 264. See also **Suffolk**.
? Ailwy of Thetford	soon after 1066	*DB*, II, 273a, 278a, cf. Stenton, *EHR*, XXXVII (1922), 227, 233.
? Waleran	soon after 1066	Ruin caused to burgesses of Norwich 'partly because of fires, partly because of the king's tax, partly by Waleran': *DB*, II, 118: cf. II, 217, where he is acting as a royal agent.
	dead by 1086, possibly by 1076	Succeeded by his son or nephew John by 1086, possibly by 1076, when the latter seized the mill of Vains in Normandy, previously held by Waleran: *Complete Peerage*, XII(2), App. B.
Robert Blund	before 1086	*DB*, II, 118.
? Ivo Taillebois	1075 × 1086	Added 20 men to geld at a manor which had belonged to Earl Ralph, who lost his lands after 1075. Also enfeoffed Count Alan of land in Islington, and with others was vouched to warranty about land in Happisburgh: *DB*, II, 125b, 149, 150. Possibly involved in land distribution rather than sheriff.
Roger Bigod	? 1086	*DB*, II, 179: 'R. the sheriff' is identified in this entry as Roger Bigod, but the county concerned is not specified. As Roger was sheriff of Suffolk in 1086, it may be a reference to him in that capacity. It is not clear when Roger became sheriff of Norfolk. He may have been appointed as early as 1069: a Roger the sheriff witnesses *RRAN*, I, no. 28. This may, however, be another Roger or be referring to him as sheriff of Suffolk. Roger was sheriff in the early years of Henry I's reign: see below.
? Humphrey the chamberlain	1087 × 1100	*RRAN*, I, no. 448, and cf. II, 403 = B & C, no. 18 (1095).
? H[ermer] de Ferrers and ? Godric *dapifer*	1091 × 1100	*RRAN*, I, no. 461.
with Goscelin		*RRAN*, I, no. 392.

Ralph de Beaufou	occ. 1091 × 1102	*Cart. Ram.*, I, 149, states that Ralph was sheriff in the time of Abbot Aldwin of Ramsey, viz 1091–1102, but does not say whether the county concerned was Norfolk or Suffolk.
Roger Bigod	1100, apparently until his death in 1107	*RRAN*, II, no. 509 (1100) describes him explicitly as sheriff of Norfolk and Suffolk. For other possible references see index to *RRAN*, II. Described as *custos* of Norfolk 1104 × 1107: *First Register of Norwich Cathedral Priory*, p. 32. For date of Roger's death: OV, VI, 144–6.
Ralph de Beaufou	occ. 1108 × 1115, c. 1110, 1107 × 1111	*RRAN*, II, nos. 875, 946, 954.
? Ralph Passelewe	1107 × 1116, 1114 × 1121	Ralph was sheriff of Suffolk in the early years of Henry I's reign. He occurs in two documents concerning Norfolk but in both is addressed second, after (respectively) William Bigod and Robert FitzWalter, who may have been sheriffs at the time: *RRAN*, II, nos. 1036, 1306.
? William Bigod	occ. 1114 1107 × 1116, 1114 × 1120	*RRAN*, II, nos. 1064, 1067. *RRAN*, II, no. 1036; *Cart. Ram.*, I, 149. William died in 1120: OV, VI, 304.
Robert FitzWalter	? 1115–1129: described as sheriff 1121 × 1127, 1123 × Mich 1129, 1121 × 1148	*RRAN*, II, nos. 1461, 1597, 1598; for other possible references, see index to *RRAN*, II; *PR 31 Henry I*, p. 90. Grant by Abbot Anselm of Bury to Robert with witnesses *ex parte vicecomitis*: *FDBSE*, no. 125, p. 123. Lived on into Stephen's reign: Round, *EHR*, XXXV (1920), 483–6. It is not certain that he was ever sheriff again in Norfolk, but is described as a justice with Aubrey de Vere: *RRAN*, II, no. 1714. Green, *Government of England under Henry I*, p. 66.
Richard Basset and Aubrey de Vere	1129–1130	*PR 31 Henry I*, p. 90.
? Fulkwinus de Fontains	1127 × 1134	*St Benet of Holme*, I, 173–4. County not specified but concerns Norfolk; cf. II, 192, where it is suggested this man is to be identified with Fulk, sheriff of Cambridgeshire, Huntingdonshire and Surrey.
John de Chesney	occ. 1140, 1144, 1146 1141 × 1146 1144, 1146	Witnessed Stephen's charter for St Benet: *RRAN*, III, no. 399. For a reference earlier than 1140, possibly as sheriff of Suffolk, see under that county. John the sheriff witnessed a grant in Mancroft, Norwich, by abbot of St Benet: *St Benet of Holme*, I, 81. Jessopp and James, *St William of Norwich*, pp. 29, 111–12. Thought to have died in 1146: Round, *EHR*, XXXV (1920), 486–7.

? Wymerus Caperun	? 1140 × 1146	The chronicler of St Benet described him as sheriff of Norfolk when Hugh was appointed abbot of St Benet, viz at a date before 1146: John of Oxenedes, *Chronica*, p. 295; *St Benet of Holme*, II, 195–6, and extract there cited. It seems likely, however, that this is a reference to Wymer *capellanus*, sheriff later in the twelfth century.
William de Chesney	1146 × 1149 1146 × 1153	*RRAN*, III, no. 401. Jessopp and James, *St William of Norwich*, pp. xxxiv, 128, 172.
? Roger Gulafre	1148 × 1153	Roger and William Frehnei (Fresney) sheriffs when a joint shire court of Norfolk and Suffolk held. The latter was sheriff of Suffolk, so Roger was presumably sheriff of Norfolk, though the two may have been joint sheriffs: Cam, *EHR*, XXXIX (1924), 571.
William	1150 1153 × 1154	Jessopp and James, *St William of Norwich*, p. 172. Writ of Stephen addressed to W. bishop of Norwich, Rainald de Warenne, and William of Norwich – presumably the sheriff, as sheriffs sometimes took their names from the principal boroughs of their counties: *RRAN*, III, no. 403.
Earl Hugh	1154–1155	*RBE*, II, 651.
William de Neville	before Mich 1155 1155–1156	Accounts for the old farm at Michaelmas 1156, *PR 2–4 Henry II*, p. 6.

Northamptonshire

Northman	1053 × 1066	Harmer, no. 94 = S 1138, cf. no. 62 (1055 × 1065) = S 1110 (according to editor 'not authentic but the address may have been taken from an authentic writ').
William de Cahagnes	1070 × 1087 1103 × 1106	*RRAN*, I, no. 288b, and possible references nos. 383 (1087 × 1096), 476 (1094 × 1100); II, no. 694, and possible references nos. 732, 770.
Robert de Pavilli	1103 × 1106	*RRAN*, II, nos. 743, 744. 743 is a notification by Queen Matilda addressed to the abbot of Peterborough, Earl Simon, Robert de Pavilli, sheriff, Michael of Hanslope and all of Northamptonshire about the grant of Tixover (Rutland); 744 is the king's notification on the same matter addressed to the abbot of Peterborough, S. Earl, Michael of Hanslope, Robert de Pavilli and all of Northamptonshire. Michael of Hanslope was castellan of Rockingham, and it would appear that it was in this capacity that he was addressed in both documents. Robert may also have been sheriff of Leicestershire.
Hugh the priest	1100 × 1112 but presumably *post* 1106	Witnessed the settlement of a lawsuit: CUL Addit. MS 2021, ff. 414v, 415, the latter printed in Stenton, *English Justice*, p. 139.
Hugh	occ. between 1106 and 1128 1107 × 1123 prob. c. 1109 1109 × 1120	*RRAN*, II, nos. 849 (1107), 887 (1107 × 1108), 996 (1106 × 1111), 997 (1107 × 1111); *English Episcopal Acta*, I, no. 8, pp. 7–8. *English Episcopal Acta*, I, no. 7, p. 7: a notification of Bishop Robert addressed to archdeacon Robert, Hugh the sheriff, Gosfrid Ridel, Walter of Hanslope, Walter Ponhar and the parishioners of Northamptonshire.
Hugh of Leicester	1106 × 1116 1107 × 1111 1107 × 1116 1121 c. 1113 × 1123 before Mich 1129	*RRAN*, II, no. 755, addressed to Hugh of Leicester and Geoffrey Ridel, and no. 975, addressed to Hugh of Leicester, Geoffrey Ridel, and Aubrey the chamberlain. In theory it is possible that Geoffrey Ridel was sheriff, but clearly Hugh of Leicester is to be identified with Hugh the sheriff and Hugh the priest of the preceding entries. If Geoffrey is not being addressed as a local magnate he may have been a local justiciar. *RRAN*, II, nos. 1032, 1244, 1409, and see also no. 1410. In none of these is Hugh explicitly stated to be sheriff, but the form of nos. 1032 and 1244 leaves no doubt that he held this office. *PR 31 Henry I*, p. 81.

Hugh de Warelville	Mich 1129–Easter 1130	*PR 31 Henry I*, p. 85.
Richard Basset and Aubrey de Vere	Easter–Mich 1130	*PR 31 Henry I*, p. 81.
Robert Grimbald	1136 × 1153, 1154–1155	*RRAN*, III, no. 611. *RBE*, II, 655.

Northumberland

[handwritten: Sheriff of Bamburgh (hereditary) and Corbridge (probably hereditary?) c. 1100 — 1150]

No evidence has been found of royal sheriffs before 1095.[1] William the Conqueror continued his predecessors' practice of appointing earls to rule in the region, albeit with little success in terms of effective control. After the rebellion of Earl Waltheof in 1075, Bishop Walcher of Durham fulfilled the function of earl, and it is in his time that the first references to a sheriff appear. Bishop Walcher was murdered in 1080; he was succeeded as earl by Robert de Mowbray, and Morel may have been his sheriff. Robert rebelled in 1095, and his lands were confiscated. No further attempts were made to rule through earls, and royal sheriffs begin to appear instead. For the sheriffs see Blair, *Archaeologia Aeliana*, 4th series, XX (1942), pp. 24–6.

? Gilbert	before 1080	Said to have been a kinsman of Bishop Walcher, under whom he ruled the 'county of the Northumbrians'. Gilbert killed a man named Liulf, and in reprisal both he and the bishop were killed: SD, II, 209–10. Gilbert, nephew of the bishop, attests a charter of Bishop Walcher (1074 × 1075): *Durham Episcopal Charters*, no. 5a, pp. 45–6.
? Morel	before 1095	Kinsman of Robert de Mowbray, and involved in the rebellion of 1095: SD, II, 226; Morel the sheriff attests purported grant and confirmation by Bishop William of Durham, 1091 × 1092: *Durham Episcopal Charters*, no. 6, pp. 48–53.
? Robert Picot	1095	*RRAN*, I, no. 367.
? Roger Picot	occ. between 1101 and 1106	*RRAN*, II, nos. 572 (1102 × 1106), 589 (1102), 624 (1102 ?), 671 (1101 × 1104).
? Robert de Lacy	1102 × 1106	*RRAN*, II, no. 631. Wightman, *Lacy Family*, p. 65, points out that the form *vicecomes de Laceio* 'is spurious, and does not of itself give much weight to the suggestion that he was the sheriff of Northumberland'. This royal notification was addressed to Gerard, archbishop of York, Robert de Lacy and Roger Picot; the last-named may have been the sheriff.
Aluric of Corbridge and Odard of Bamburgh	occ. between c. 1103 and 1116	*RRAN*, II, nos. 640 (c. 1103 × 1108), 641 (c. 1103), 955, 993, 1143, 1172 (1107 × 1116), and for other possible references, see index.
Odard of Bamburgh	occ. between 1115 and 1130	*RRAN*, II, nos. 1124 (1116), 1202 (1115 × 1119), 1264 (1120 × 1133), 1279 (1115 × 1127), 1339 (c. 1116 × c. 1126), 1563 (1118 × 1128); *PR 31 Henry I*, p. 35.
Adam son of Odard	occ. between c. 1133 and c. 1147	Blair, *Archaeologia Aeliana*, 4th series, XX (1942), 25–6.

[handwritten note above Aluric row: Liulf (son of Eadwulf)]

[handwritten note under Odard of Bamburgh: son of Liulf]

[handwritten note at bottom: Adam s. 'Edward' (w) Lawrie, Charters, no. 100.]

1. For background see Kapelle, *The Norman Conquest of the North*, pp. 11–13.

Robert Bertram occ. 1139 × 1152 Attests as sheriff (county not specified) notification by
? after 1147 Prince Henry of Scotland for Tynemouth priory. The
limits of dating are thus those of Henry's tenure of the
earldom: *Regesta Regum Scottorum*, I, no. 27; also
witnesses nos. 11 (1139 × 1142), 32 (1141 × 1151).
For further details about Robert: Hedley,
Northumberland Families, I, 191.

Nottinghamshire

This county was probably held jointly with Derbyshire, *q.v.*

Hugh FitzBaldric	1066 × 1086	*DB*, I, 260. Still living 1089 when witnessed charter for Duke Robert: *Early Yorkshire Charters*, IX, xii.
? Hugh de Port	1086 × 1096, 1087 before 9 Sept	*RRAN*, I, nos. 381, 382 = B & C, no. 27. Both relate to Rutland, where Hugh de Port held two royal estates at farm.
	1080 × 1087	*RRAN*, I, no. 275, also relates to Rutland, but is addressed to Remigius, bishop of Lincoln, Hugh de Port and all of Nottinghamshire; it may not be genuine as the churches mentioned as having been granted to Westminster abbey are not mentioned in *DB*. May have been farmer of Rutland rather than sheriff of Nottinghamshire: Adams, *Mercian Studies*, pp. 68–9.
? Earnwig	occ. between 1075 and 1092	*RRAN*, I, no. 333, addressed to Thomas the archbishop of York, and Turold and Earnwig his sheriff (or sheriffs) and all his thanes in Nottinghamshire and Lincolnshire; no. 335 is similarly addressed and both suggest that Turold was sheriff of Nottinghamshire and Earnwig of Lincolnshire. However, Turold was sheriff of Lincolnshire (see under that county) so Earnwig was probably sheriff of Nottinghamshire. Cf. no. 337 addressed to Thomas the archbishop, Earl Roger, E. the sheriff, H. de Ferrers, W. Peverel, and all his lieges, French and English, of Nottinghamshire and Derbyshire. E. was presumably Earnwig of Nottinghamshire and Derbyshire.
	1093	
? William Peverel	1086 × 1100	*RRAN*, I, No. 438, a royal notification addressed to the archbishop of York, William Peverel and all of Nottinghamshire. The churches confirmed to Durham in this notification were still in the king's hands in 1086.
R.	1100 × 1102	*RRAN*, II, nos. 502 (1100), 538 (1101 × 1102).
? Richard son of Gotse	1101 × 1107, 1102	Possibly addressed as sheriff of Nottinghamshire in two documents about Blyth: *RRAN*, II, nos. 588, 598.
Richard (presumably R. son of Gotse)	1101 × 1103 or 1105	*RRAN*, II, no. 720.
Richard son of Gotse	1101 × 1107	*RRAN*, II, no. 870.
Helgot	1100 × 1108, 1105	*RRAN*, II, nos. 704, 705.
Robert de Heriz	1110 × 1122	*RRAN*, II, no. 1355.

The following four sheriffs are known to have held Nottinghamshire with Derbyshire:

Serlo de Burg	before 1127	*PR 31 Henry I*, p. 31.
Ivo de Heriz	1127–1128	*PR 31 Henry I*, p. 7.
Osbert Salvain	1128 – Easter 1130	*PR 31 Henry I*, pp. 6–7.
Robert de Perer	1154–1155	*RBE*, II, 653.

Oxfordshire

Edwin	before 1086, possibly before 1066	Henry de Ferrers, *DB* tenant of Dene and Chalford, bought three hides of land from Edwin the sheriff: *DB*, I, 157b. The transaction took place after 1066 but it is not clear whether Edwin was still sheriff at the time.
Alwi (Aelfwig)	?	Alwi the sheriff holds (present tense) 2½ hides in Bletchingdon, which Manasses is said to have bought from him without the king's licence: *DB*, I, 160b. Possibly to be identified with Aluui of Gloucestershire.
Swawold	c. 1067	*RRAN*, I, no. 18.
? Roger	1069	*RRAN*, I, no. 28 (see above under **Devon**).
? Robert d'Oilly	c. 1071	*RRAN*, I, no. 49, and see **Berkshire**.
Swein	? 1086	Swein the sheriff held a manor at Toot Baldon in chief: *DB*, I, 154. He may have been Swein, sheriff of Essex. There is insufficient evidence relating to the subsequent descent of this manor to confirm the identification: *VCH Oxfordshire*, V, 50.
Peter	1087 × 1097, 1093 × 1100	*RRAN*, I, nos. 390, 466; *Chron. Abingdon*, II, 41, and mentioned 153.
William	occ. between 1100 and 1110	*RRAN*, II, nos. 527 (1101 ?), 693 (1101 × 1105), 699 (1101 × 1105), 726 (1100 × 1110), 758 (1106), 813 (1107), 814, 815 (? 1107), 816 (1107), 854 (1100 × 1107), 937 (1107 × 1110); witnesses with King Henry a gift by Robert FitzHaimon: *Chron. Abingdon*, II, 96–7.
W. (presumably William)	1105, 1100 × 1107, 1100 × 1108	*RRAN*, II, nos. 700, 708, 724.
Thomas of St John with Richard de Monte	5 Aug 1110 × 5 Aug 1111	*Chron. Abingdon*, II, 119.
? Thomas of St John	1111, 1113 × 1116	Thomas was also addressed in three other documents, possibly as sheriff: *RRAN*, II, nos. 973, 1000, 1128; the last is addressed to Robert, bishop of Lincoln, Thomas of St John, Nigel d'Oilly, and all the barons of
? Nigel d'Oilly	1113 × 1116	Oxfordshire. Nigel thus may have been sheriff.
? Richard de Monte	1110 × 1117, 1110 × 1116	Richard also occurs in the address clauses of three documents, apparently as sheriff: *RRAN*, II, nos. 1053, 1132, 1133; however, doubts about the authenticity of the former are expressed by Clanchy, *From Memory to Written Record*, pp. 107–8.

Restold	1122 × 1127 before Mich 1127	*Cart. St Frideswide*, I, 22. *RRAN*, II, nos. 1470 (1126 × 1127), 1528 (1118 × 1127). Restold seems to have left office at Mich 1127, as his successor had held Garsington at farm for at least two years before Mich 1129: *PR 31 Henry I*, pp. 1–2. Also occurs in *Chron. Abingdon*, II, 184–5.
Robert (probably Robert d'Oilly)	? 1128–1129 1129–1130	*PR 31 Henry I*, pp. 1–2, 6. Top of membrane with sheriff's name is missing. Second entry begins *Et idem Robertus*, as does the third which includes a debt *patris sui pro pecunia Widonis de Oilli*. Robert d'Oilly was pardoned £7 16s. danegeld in 1130.
Azor	1147	Witnessed a charter of William de Chesney of 1147: *Cart. Oseney*, IV, 87; also (as Azor the sheriff) charter of Aliz de Langetot 1142 × 1148: *Cart. Eynsham*, I, 104. Mentioned as former sheriff of Oxfordshire: *Cart. Eynsham*, II, 43.
John	c. 1150 × 1160	*Cart. St Frideswide*, II, 297–8. May have preceded Henry, as no sheriff of this name occurs after 1154. Perhaps John of St John.
Henry of Oxford	1153, 1154–1155	*RRAN*, III, no. 13; *RBE*, II, 657.

Shropshire

No pre-Conquest sheriffs have been identified. In 1071 the county was given to Roger of Montgomery, and he and his two sons, Hugh and Robert, are thought to have controlled the shrievalty until Robert's downfall in 1102.[1] The evidence about successive sheriffs suggests that for some decades there were holders of the fee of Warin, the first Norman sheriff, who called themselves sheriffs, and other men who, also calling themselves sheriffs, actually did the work. At a later date the latter would have been described as under-sheriffs, but the term has been avoided below, because the men concerned seem rather to have been deputies for men with hereditary claims to a baronial shrievalty than under-sheriffs of the later type. The lands and office of Warin passed to Renaud de Bailleul, possibly to Warin's son Hugh, and finally to Alan FitzFlaald.[2] Renaud was evidently sheriff in 1086, and Alan was described as sheriff in Henry II's confirmation of a gift to Shrewsbury abbey (see list, below). Arthur the sheriff who is mentioned in 1085 or 1086 may thus have been Renaud's deputy, succeeded later by Fulk the sheriff who first occurs between 1094 and 1098 and was still living in 1121 if not later. Meanwhile Robert de Bellême lost Shropshire with his other estates in 1102 and Renaud de Bailleul seems to have retired to his Norman estates.[3] Overall charge of the county was given to Richard de Beaumais, formerly a clerk in Earl Roger's household, and, from 1108, bishop of London.[4] Richard is not described explicitly as sheriff, and it may have been that Fulk was his acting deputy until the bishop's retirement in 1126, to be succeeded in the county by Payn FitzJohn.

Warin	1081, 1085	RRAN, I, no. 140; OV, III, 234, 240; Galbraith, EHR, XLIV (1929), 372. Benefactor of Shrewsbury abbey: Cart. Shrewsbury, I, no. 34, p. 30.
Arthur	1086	Eyton, Antiquities of Shropshire I, 112; Mason, Transactions of the Shropshire Archaeological Society LVI (1957–60), 247. Renaud is said to have been sheriff in 1086, and to have held Warin's lands. Arthur could either have been sheriff for a brief period after Warin's death, or acting sheriff, subordinate to Renaud.
Renaud de Bailleul	1086	Married Warin's widow Amieria: Mon. Ang., III, 518. Niece of Earl Roger: OV, II, 262; succeeded to Warin's estates and office: DB, I, 254; Eyton, Antiquities of Shropshire, II, 193 ff.
	1098	CDF, no. 666, pp. 237–8.
? Hugh, son of Warin	? possibly after 1102	Eyton, Antiquities of Shropshire, VII, 210, 211. Seems to have held his father's lands, and possibly his office for a short time, perhaps after Renaud's departure from England, although there are no indications that Fulk ceased to be acting sheriff.

1. For the family see: Mason, *Transactions of the Royal Historical Society*, 5th series, XIII (1963), 1–28. For the early sheriffs see: Mason, *Transactions of the Shropshire Archaeological Society*, LVI (1957–1960), 244–7; Eyton, *Antiquities of Shropshire*, VII, 202–11.
2. Eyton, *Antiquities of Shropshire*, VII, 202–23.
3. Orderic Vitalis mentions Renaud's rebellion against Henry I in 1119, and that he took part in an expedition to Spain: VI, 214, 402.
4. Mason, *Transactions of the Shropshire Archaeological Society*, LVI (1957–60), 253–4.

Fulk (acting sheriff, see introductory note above)	1094 × 1098 (1094–1098)	Attested charter of Earl Hugh for Shrewsbury abbey and described as a 'baron' of the county in Henry I's confirmation of 1121 which he also attested: *Cart. Shrewsbury*, I, no. 4, p. 10 and no. 35, pp. 35, 36; possibly to be identified with Fulk, *DB*, I, 259b. May have been Renaud's deputy before 1102.
	1102	*RRAN*, II, no. 618: addressed to Richard de Beaumais and Fulk the sheriff.
	occ. 1121	Witnessed two documents issued by Henry I: *Cart. Shrewsbury*, I, no. 35, p. 36 (mentioned above) and no. 47b, p. 52 = *RRAN*, II, no. 1299.
	occ. 1135 × 1138	Benefactor of Shrewsbury abbey: *Cart. Shrewsbury*, I, no. 40, pp. 47–8; II, no. 257, 258, 262–3; Mason, *Transactions of the Shropshire Archaeological Society*, LVI (1957–60), 247.
? Alan [FitzFlaald]	before 1114	Described as sheriff (county not specified) in charter of Henry II confirming donations to Shrewsbury abbey: *Cart. Shrewsbury*, I, no. 36, pp. 42, 45. In Henry I's confirmation Alan confirmed his predecessor's gifts, but was not styled sheriff at that time: *Cart. Shrewsbury*, I, no. 35, p. 34. Had been granted the estates formerly held by Warin and Renaud and possibly claimed the office as a result: see introduction.
? Richard de Beaumais	1102 × 1126	In charge of the Montgomery estates and evidently the king's agent in the county, with the power if not the title of sheriff: *RRAN*, II, nos. 618, 1473.
? Payn FitzJohn	after 1126	*RRAN*, II, no. 1473.
	soon after 16 Jan. 1127	Notification of William, archbishop of Canterbury addressed to Payn FitzJohn and all his barons of Shropshire: *Cart. Shrewsbury*, I, no. 23, pp. 23–4.
	c. 1135	Writ of Henry I addressed to Payn FitzJohn and his ministers of Shropshire and Herefordshire: *Cart. Worc.*, no. 53, not calendared in *RRAN*.
	d. 1137	JW, p. 43.
William FitzAlan	1138	Mentioned as sheriff at time of his revolt against Stephen. He fled from Shrewsbury after Stephen besieged him there: OV, VI, 520. It is not clear what happened afterwards. Two documents issued by the Empress Matilda suggest that he was back in authority there some time later in the reign:
	? 1141 × 1143	*RRAN*, III, nos. 378,
	? 1148	461. Henry II formally restored William to his lands in 1155: Eyton, *Antiquities of Shropshire*, VII, 234–7.
	(part of) 1154–1155	*RBE*, II, 653.
	d. 1160	*PR 6 Henry II*, p. 27.

Somerset

Godwin	1060 × 1066	Harmer, nos. 64–7 = S 1111–14.
Tofi	1061 × 1066	Harmer, nos. 68 = S 1115, 69 = S 1116, 70 = S 1240, 71 = S 1263, cf. *DB*, I, 98b.
	1061 × 1082	Harmer, no. 68.
	1066 × 1082	*RRAN*, I, no. 160.
	1067	*RRAN*, I, no. 7; see also no. 23.
? William de Courseulles	1076 × 1083	*RRAN*, I, no. 187. Dead by 1086: Loyd, *Anglo-Norman Families*, p. 33.
William de Mohun	1066 × 1083	Addressed as sheriff in a writ of Queen Matilda instructing him to give Bishop Giso seisin of the church of Wedmore: Wells, Dean and Chapter, 'Liber Albus', f. 58r, calendared *HMC Wells*, I, 66.
William	1086	William the sheriff was allowed £12 in his farm for Wedmore, which had been granted to Bishop Giso before 1066 but was listed in 1086 under the *Terra Regis* as well as under Giso's land: *DB*, I, 86b. Exon Domesday reveals that William de Mohun held royal manors at farm: *DB*, IV, 103 (Old Cleeve), 104 (Winsford), and this in turn increases the likelihood that he was the William who held other royal manors at farm. But note that one William Huse had 'received' (i.e. been granted the farm of) the royal manor of Keynsham: *DB*, IV, 113. William and Walter Huse were both landholders in 1086; Walter may have been sheriff later: see below.
Aiulf	1089 × 1091, 1088 × 1100	*RRAN*, I, nos. 326 (possibly with Wiltshire), 457, and see also no. 315.
William Capra	1091 × 1096	*RRAN*, II, 404.
Aiulf	occ. 1100 × 1108	*RRAN*, II, 622 (1100 × 1102), 735 (1102 × 1105), 763 (1100 × 1107), 896 (1100 × 1108).
? Walter Huse	1106	Witnessed a charter of John, bishop of Bath: *Two Chartularies . . . of Bruton*, p. 52.
Robert de Gornay	1106 × 1122	*RRAN*, II, no. 989 (editors have misread Gornay as Gerreton: Barrow, *Scottish Historical Review*, XXXVI (1957), 61).
? Richard FitzBaldwin	1107 × 1122	*RRAN*, II, no. 1368.

Warin	1122, 1121 × 1124, 1110 × 1129	*RRAN*, II, nos. 1341 (with Dorset), 1364, 1384; mentioned in BL Cotton MS Cleopatra C VII, f. 100r-v, one of a series of charters in a cartulary of Merton priory relating to Bernard the scribe and thought to date from c. 1130.
	? 1130	There is no separate account for Somerset in the 1130 pipe roll. Warin was sheriff of Dorset and Somerset in 1130 and accounted for the old farm of three counties, so the third was presumably Somerset, *PR 31 Henry I*, p. 12. He was still living at the start of Stephen's reign: see under **Dorset**.
Richard of Montacute	(half of) 1154– 1155	*RBE*, II, 654.

Staffordshire

? Aevic	in reign of Cnut	Sheriff when Worcester cathedral priory's possession of Swinford (Staffs), Tardebigge, and Clent (Worcs) was contested: *Hemingi Chartularium*, I, 277, 278. Not clear, therefore, whether sheriff of Staffordshire or Worcestershire.
Thurkill	1066 × 1068	*RRAN*, I, no. 25.
R.	1074 × 1085	*RRAN*, I, no. 210. Possibly Robert of Stafford, a leading landholder in the county in 1086.
? Nicholas	1086	'Nigel holds 3 hides in Kingsley which Nicholas claims as belonging to the king's farm in Clifton': *DB*, I, 250b. As Clifton was a royal manor, Nicholas may have been sheriff. Robert of Stafford (of the Tosny family) had a son named Nicholas who succeeded to his father's lands c. 1088, but it is not clear whether the son was Nicholas the sheriff or the sheriff was Nicholas de Beauchamp. The latter was not a tenant-in-chief in 1086: *Complete Peerage*, XII(2), App. F.
N.	1088 × 1100	*RRAN*, I, no. 456. Possibly Nicholas.
? Ger' of Kinver	1100 × 1130	Addressed in a writ of Henry I, possibly as sheriff: *Cart. Worc.*, no. 24, p. 19 (not calendared in *RRAN*, II).
Nicholas of Stafford	occ. between 1101 and 1123	*RRAN*, II, nos. 600 (1100 × 1102), 766 (1101 × 1106), 900 (1101 × 1102), 1054 (1114?), 1412 (1107 × 1123 as N.). Land of the mother of Nicholas sheriff of Stafford is mentioned in 1130: *PR 31 Henry I*, p. 82.
Robert of Stanley	1123–1128	*PR 31 Henry I*, p. 73.
Miles of Gloucester	1128–1130	*PR 31 Henry I*, p. 72.
? Philip de Beaumais	1136 × 1140	*RRAN*, III, no. 966. Stephen addresses Waleran count of Meulan, Philip de Beaumais, and all his ministers of Worcestershire and Staffordshire. Editor suggests Philip apparently sheriff of Staffordshire, perhaps on grounds that William de Beauchamp may have been sheriff of Worcestershire.
Robert of Stafford	? 1136 × 1148	Robert the sheriff (county not specified) witnessed Geva Ridel's foundation charter for Canwell priory: *Mon. Ang.*, IV, 105. This was issued after the death of Richard Basset (living in 1136: OV, VI, 468) and before the death of Roger, bishop of Chester.
	1154–1155	*RBE*, II, 652.
? Maurice	occ. 1156	Possibly deputy to Robert, sheriff 1155–1156: *PR 2–4 Henry II*, pp. 29, 30. Presumably the man identified by Wedgwood, *Collections for a History of Staffordshire*, 3rd series (1912), 274, as Maurice Tiretei (sheriff of Essex).

Suffolk

? Leofstan	940 × 970	A wicked sheriff mentioned in an account written in the late eleventh century of the miracles of St Edmund: *Memorials of St Edmund's Abbey*, I, 30–2.
? Toli	1052, 1053 × 1057 1065 × 1066	Harmer, nos. 10 = S 1070, 18 = S 1084, 20 = S 1080. None mention which was Toli's county, but all are for Bury. Cf. nos. 23 = S 1083, 24 = S 1084, 25 = S 1085, also for Bury, and including Toli in the address without, however, describing him as sheriff. Mentioned *DB*, II, 299b, 334, 338, 409b.
Norman	before 1086 1066 × 1070	*RRAN*, I, no. 40. Held land TRE: *DB*, II, 312b, 334b. Still living 1086: *DB*, II, 327, 438. In a position of authority when King William instructed him to put Ralph de Savenai in seisin of freemen of whom Hubert de Port had previously put 'the bishop' (Odo of Bayeux) in seisin: Norman had accordingly put Ralph in seisin. The land concerned was still in dispute in 1086: *DB*, II, 377.
? William Malet	1066 × 1070	*RRAN*, I, no. 44, but see II, p. 391: the Cambridge MSS give Robert Malet as the addressee.
Robert Malet	1071	*RRAN*, I, no. 47.
Roger Bigod	? 1072 × 1075	Mentioned as having soke in the 5½ Suffolk hundreds of Ely abbey: *Inquisitio Comitatus Cantabrigiensis*, p. 194. Preceded Robert Malet: *DB*, II, 287b.
Robert Malet	1080	*RRAN*, I, no. 122.
Roger Bigod	1086	*DB*, II, 282, 292b, 393 (as Roger); *VCH Suffolk*, I, 389.
? Godric *dapifer*	1087, 1087 × 1097	*RRAN*, I, nos. 291, 392.
? Humphrey the chamberlain	1087 × 1096	*RRAN*, II, 403 = B & C, no. 18 (? 1095).
? Ralph de Beaufou	1091 × 1109	*Curt. Rum.*, I, 149.
? Robert Malet	1102 × 1105, 1101 × 1106	*RRAN*, II, nos. 655, 700.
Roger Bigod	1101 × 1107, 1103 × 1106, 1106	*RRAN*, II, nos. 588, 738, 791.
? Ralph Passelewe	occ. between 1100 and 1107	*RRAN*, II, nos. 591 (1102, addressed to Roger Bigod, Ralph Passelewe and all of Norfolk and Suffolk), 740 (1104 × 1107, to R. Bigod, R. Passelewe, and the king's liege men of Norfolk and Suffolk), 740 (1104 × 1107, to R. Bigod, R. Passelewe and their ministers and all of Norfolk and Suffolk), 760 (1104 × 1107, to Herbert the bishop, R. Bigod, R. Passelewe and their ministers and the king's lieges of Norfolk and Suffolk and Otho the goldsmith of London), 777 (1103 ×

1106, to Herbert the bishop, R. Bigod, R. Passelewe, and the barons of Norfolk and Suffolk), 786 (1104 × 1107, to R. Bigod then as 591), 787 (1104 × 1107, as 591). These address clauses suggest that Roger Bigod was sheriff of Norfolk and Ralph Passelewe of Suffolk, but there are other possibilities: the two men could have held both counties as sheriff and deputy, or Ralph could have been local justiciar: Cronne, *University of Birmingham Historical Journal*, VI (1957), 28–9.

? Hugh Lyoth	1104 × 1107	*RRAN*, II, no. 861. Possibly a mistake for Hugh of Buckland, sheriff of Essex.
? Ralph de Beaufou	1101 × 1106, 1107 × 1116, 1106 × 1116	*RRAN*, II, nos. 780, 932, 1144, and note also no. 1049.
? William Bigod	c. 1114	*RRAN*, II, no. 1067.
Robert FitzWalter	occ. between 1108 and 1129	*RRAN*, II, nos. 1218 (1108 × 1119, concerns Suffolk), 1219 (1108 × 1119), 1321 (1121 × 1122), 1461 (1121 × 1127, with Norfolk), 1597 (1123 × 1129, with Norfolk, and styled simply as Robert), 1598 (1123 × 1129, with Norfolk), and for other possible references, see index to *RRAN*, II; *Cart. Ram.*, I, 148–9;
	1128–1129	*PR 31 Henry I*, p. 90. Still living in Stephen's reign, see under **Norfolk**.
Richard Basset and Aubrey de Vere	1129–1130	*PR 31 Henry I*, p. 90.
John son of Robert FitzWalter	1137 × 1138	John FitzRobert the sheriff (county not specified) attested confirmation for Eye: *RRAN*, III, no. 288. It is clear from the *narratio fundationis* of Sibton abbey that John was the son of Robert FitzWalter. This text describes John as 'the sheriff' (county not specified), and says that he was succeeded in his lands by his brother William de Chesney: *Sibton Abbey Cartularies*, II, 9. It seems likely that both John and William were sheriffs of Suffolk as well as Norfolk. John occurs as sheriff of Norfolk between 1140 and 1146.
William de Chesney	concurrently with Norfolk, 1146 × 1153	See note for preceding entry.
William de Fresney	before 1155 ? Mich 1154 – Easter 1155	Accounts at Mich 1156 for the old farm of the preceding year: *PR 2–4 Henry II*, p. 8.
Earl Hugh	1154–1155 for half of the year ? Easter-Mich 1155	*RBE*, II, 652.

Surrey

Ansculf de Picquigny	1066 × 1086	*DB*, I, 36. Dead by 1086, by which date he had evidently been succeeded by his son William: *DB*, I, 35b, 36, 148b.
O.	1070 × 1082	*RRAN*, I, no. 162. A note suggests O. may have been a mistake, but cf. no. 417.
Ranulf	1086	*DB*, I. 30, 32; Green, *Anglo-Norman Studies*, V (1983), 135, for the suggestion that this was Rannulf Flambard. If, however, Ranulf is to be identified with the men in the three entries following, he was not Rannulf Flambard, who was appointed bishop of Durham in 1099.
R.	1087, before 9 Sept	*RRAN*, I, no. 236, where a note states incorrectly that the copy of this writ in London, Westminster Abbey Muniment Book II, f. 174b, reads O. the sheriff. The cartulary copy also reads R. The original writ was edited B & C, no. 26. See also *RRAN*, I, no. 214 (1078 × 1095).
Rannulf	1093 × 1107	Sheriff (evidently of Surrey) in a charter of Gilbert FitzRichard, lord of Tonbridge: Kent CRO DRc/T373.
Ralph FitzNigel	1103 × 1106	*RRAN*, II, no. 639.
? Wymond	? 1085 × 1118	Addressed in will of Gilbert Crispin, abbot of Westminster (? 1085–1117 × 1118): BL Cotton MS Faustina A III, f. 259, printed *Mon. Ang.*, I, 310.
Roger	1102 × 1106	BL Harley MS 4757, f. 3: confirmation of Henry I for Bermondsey abbey addressed to Roger, sheriff of Surrey and G. his nephew (? Gilbert the knight). Dated by the appearance of Waldric the chancellor. Not in *RRAN*, II,
	1103 × 1104	*RRAN*, II, no. 664.
Gilbert the knight	occ. between 1103 and 1125	*RRAN*, II, nos. 659 (1103 × 1106), 851 (1103 × 1107), 1350 (1107 × 1122), 1416 (1123 × 1126, county not specified but concerns Surrey), 1435 (1121 × 1135); for date of death: *Records of Merton Priory*, p. 5.
	1114 × 1119	*Chron. Ram.*, I, 238; *Cart. Ram.*, I, 131;
	1122	*Chron. Ram.*, I, 248.
Fulk nephew of Gilbert	1126, 1127, 1128–1129	*Cart. Colchester*, I, p. 78; Round, *Commune of London*, pp. 121–2; *PR 31 Henry I*, p. 44.
Richard Basset and Aubrey de Vere	1129–1130	*PR 31 Henry I*, p. 43.

Ralph	before 1140	Ralph the sheriff gave land in Surrey to Waverley, the gift being confirmed in 1140: *RRAN*, III, no. 921. Possibly to be identified with Ralph, sheriff of Cambridgeshire and/or Ranulf of London.
Payn	? 1139 × 1154	Describes himself as sheriff of Surrey: BL Cotton MS Domitian A X, f. 143v. This is presumably Payn of Hemingford, sheriff of Cambridgeshire and Huntingdonshire during Stephen's reign, who occurs between 1139 and 1154.
	1155–1156	Accounts (? as deputy) on behalf of William Martel: *PR 2–4 Henry II*, p. 10.
? William Martel	1135 × 1154, 1154–1155	*RRAN*, III, no. 934; *RBE*, II, 654.

Sussex

It is not certain whether there were royal sheriffs before the reign of Henry I. William the Conqueror retained little demesne land here, granting out the rest as compact territorial lordships called rapes.[1] Each had its own sheriff subordinate to the lord of the rape. By 1129–1130, however, there was an agent, presumably a sheriff, accounting at the Exchequer. In the intervening period two of the rapes had been confiscated, Arundel in 1102 and Pevensey in 1104, as a result of rebellion by their lords against Henry I. Arundel was retained by the crown until granted in dower to Adeliza, widow of Henry I, who married William d'Aubigny in 1138.[2] Part of Pevensey was held by Gilbert de l'Aigle, then at intervals was held by Richer de l'Aigle, and Earl Gilbert of Pembroke.[3] In 1147 King Stephen captured Pevensey castle and granted it to his son William. Whilst in private hands each of the rapes had their own sheriffs, but at some stage sheriffs for the county started to be appointed. The earliest[4] may have been Hugh de Warelville in 1129–1130, but he is not explicitly called sheriff, and a clear sequence only begins with the bishop of Chichester in 1155.

Sheriffs of the County

? William son of Wibert		*PRO Revised List*, p. 141, without source. This is presumably the man who was an under-tenant of the count of Eu and who was a benefactor of Battle abbey: London, Lincoln's Inn MS 87, f. 48.
? William FitzAnsger	1120	Notification addressed to Ralph, bishop of Chichester, William FitzAnsger and the barons of Sussex: *RRAN*, II, no. 1238. Presumably the man of that name said to have been granted Bosham at farm: *BF*, I, 71. Also perhaps to be identified with the man included in an address of a royal writ instructing that justice be done to the bishop of Bayeux: Haskins, *Norman Institutions*, p. 98. The index to *RRAN*, II, suggested that he may have been local justiciar. He was dead by 1122: Farrer, *Itinerary of Henry I*, no. 447 (citing Delisle, *Rouleaux des Morts*, p. 293).
Hugh de Warelville	1129–1130	*PR 31 Henry I*, p. 68.
? William de Pont de l'Arche	1133, 1107 × 1133	*RRAN*, II, nos. 1780 (concerns Chichester), 1833 (concerns Bosham). Possibly as keeper of Arundel: *PR 31 Henry I*, p. 42.
? Ailwin	1140 × 1156	Notification of Abbot Gervase of Westminster (1140–1156) addressed to Ailwin the sheriff and all his barons of 'Southsexia': BL Cotton MS Faustina A III, f. 258b, printed *Mon. Ang.*, I, 310.

1. Mason, *William I and the Sussex Rapes*. For the descent of the rapes see Sanders, *Feudal Baronies*.
2. Sanders, *Feudal Baronies*, pp. 1–2; in 1130 Arundel was accounted for at the Exchequer by William de Pont de l'Arche: *PR 31 Henry I*, p. 42.
3. Sanders, *Feudal Baronies*, p. 136.
4. Note, however, a notification of William Rufus not calendared in *RRAN*, I, addressed to the 'bishop of Sussex' (? Chichester), and the sheriff, *Textus Roffensis*, f. 182v.

? Roger Hay	c. 1145	*PRO Revised List*, p. 141, without source. Perhaps Roger de la Haye, younger brother of William of St John and benefactor of Boxgrove, or Roger Haia, holder of forges and other property in Winchester in 1148: *VCH Sussex*, IV, 156; 1148 Survey entry nos. 90, and 38, 73, 913, 1043: Winton Domesday, *Winchester Studies*, I, 79, 74, 132, 139.
Bishop of Chichester	Jan–Mich 1155	*RBE*, II, 654.

Sheriffs of the Rapes

Arundel

Robert FitzTetbald	living 1086	Mason, *Transactions of the Shropshire Archaeological Society*, LVI (1957–60), 244–5. *Mon. Ang.*, III, 518; Mentioned: *Cart. Shrewsbury*, I, 34.
	d. 1087	*CDF*, no. 655, p. 233.

Bramber

Ralph son of Landric de Bocco	c. 1080	*Cart. Sele*, p. 2. This man is probably to be identified with Buceus *vicecomes*; note that Ralph held Kingston of William de Braose in 1086: *DB*, I, 27b.
Buceus	c. 1095 × 1115	Salter, *Facsimiles of Early Charters preserved in Oxford Muniment Rooms*, no. 1; *HMC 3rd Report*, App., p. 223. Mentioned 1096, but not as sheriff: *Cart. Sele*, p. 3. Witnessed charters of Philip de Braose (d. 1134 × 1155): London, Lincoln's Inn MS 87, ff. 70v, 71.

Chichester

? E. FitzAuger	1091 × 1100	Royal notification addressed to the bishop of Chichester, E. FitzAuger, Hoel and his other *ministris*. As the text survives only in a seventeenth-century transcript it is possible that the original read William FitzAnsger: *RRAN*, I, no. 460.

Hastings

Reinbert	occ. between 1086 and 1106	Steward and sheriff of the count of Eu: *DB*, I, 17b–19b; *RRAN*, II, nos. 691, 752.
Ingelramnus	1101, 1107 1107 × 1124 1107 × 1113 1109 × 1140	*CDF*, nos. 231, 233, pp. 80–1 (in both of these cases called Ingelran of Hastings). San Marino, Huntington Library, BA 42/1530 (as sheriff), *RRAN*, II, no. 877. San Marino, Huntington Library, BA 42/1526 (as sheriff); see also BA 42/1132 (as sheriff).
Drogo of Pevensey	occ. 1091 × 1123	*Acta of the Bishops of Chichester* no. 7, p. 75. Dead by 1130: *PR 31 Henry I*, p. 69. Described as heir of Reinbert: London, Lincoln's Inn MS 87, f. 70.
Simon son of Drogo	occ. 1130 died c. 1166	*PR 31 Henry I*, p. 69. *Acta of the Bishops of Chichester*, no. 7, p. 75.

Lewes

? Warin		Witnesses general confirmation (fabricated) of William de Warenne for Lewes priory: *Early Yorkshire Charters*, VIII, 62–4. Also printed: *Cart. Lewes*, I, 9–20.
Peter	c. 1090	*Cart. Lewes*, I, 36.
	c. 1100	*Cart. Lewes*, I, 34.
	1106 × 1118	*Early Yorkshire Charters*, VIII, 72–3. Also printed: *Cart. Lewes*, I, 40, where dated c. 1093.
	1106 × 1121	*Early Yorkshire Charters*, VIII, 73; cf. *Cart. Lewes*, I, 32–3, where dated c. 1090.
Hugh	c. 1118 × c. 1130	Addressed in mandate of William de Warenne: *Early Yorkshire Charters*, VII, 74, cf. *Cart. Lewes*, I, 39, where dated c. 1145.
William	c. 1120	*Cart. Lewes*, II, 58.
	c. 1130 × 1133	Witnessed notification of William de Warenne: *Early Yorkshire Charters*, VIII, 76, cf. *Cart. Lewes*, I, 33.
Guy de Mencecourt	1147	*Early Yorkshire Charters*, VIII, 241–2, citing PRO, E 40/15531, 15532. Charter issued by Guy dated c. 1150: *Cart. Lewes*, II, 63.
Adam	1147 × 1148	*Early Yorkshire Charters*, VIII, 97n, citing PRO, E 40/15528; cf. *Cart. Lewes*, II, 46, dated c. 1160; *Early Yorkshire Charters*, VIII, 98.
William	c. 1150	*Cart. Lewes*, II, 26.
	1154 × 1159	Douglas, *FDBSE*, no. 188; *Early Yorkshire Charters*, VIII, 241–2.

Pevensey

Gilbert	1086	*DB*, I, 20b.
Walter de Richardiville	before 1095	*CDF*, no. 1205, pp. 434–5.
? Robert	c. 1095	Robert the sheriff attests a charter of William count of Mortain concerning Pevensey: *CDF*, no. 1205, pp. 434–5.
Ranulf	before 1103 × 1106	*Cart. Lewes*, I, 119.
? Adelulf	c. 1150	Witnessed charter of Eustace, son of King Stephen, for Lewes priory. Not clear whether sheriff of Lewes or Pevensey, but sheriff of former was probably William: *Cart. Lewes*, I, 161.

Warwickshire

Edwin	before 1086, probably before 1066	Mentioned as a landholder TRE: *DB*, I, 238b, 241.
Aluuin	before 1086, possibly before 1066	Mentioned as a landholder TRE: *DB*, I, 238b, 239b. Also described as Aluuin the father of Turchil (of Warwick): *DB*, I, 241. For a man of the same name see **Gloucestershire, Herefordshire** and **Huntingdonshire.**
? Turchil of Warwick		No evidence to illustrate tenure of shrievalty, but thought to have held office because he took his name from principal borough of the county. Tenant-in-chief in 1086 and son of Alwin: *DB*, I, 240b–241b.
R.	1066 × 1077	*RRAN*, I, no. 104 (county not specified, but concerns Warwickshire). Possibly to be identified with Robert d'Oilly.
? Robert d'Oilly	1070 × 1084	*RRAN*, I, no. 200.
Walter	1079 × 1083	*RRAN*, I, no. 186. Possibly to be identified with Wal. addressed in charter (1066 × 1082) of Bishop Odo of Bayeux: Evesham Abbey Register, BL Cotton MS Vespasian B XXIV, f. 28.
? W. son of Corbucio	1095 × 1096	*RRAN*, I, no. 388.
William	1100 × 1107	*RRAN*, II, no. 654. Possibly William son of Corbucio, although in index editors suggest William de Cahagnes, sheriff of Northants.
Hugh of Leicester	1100 × 1116	*RRAN*, II, no. 1052.
H.	1107 × 1123	*RRAN*, II, no. 1412. Possibly Hugh of Leicester. Crouch, *Bulletin of the Institute of Historical Research*, LV (1982), 116, suggests Hugh may have left office in 1121.
Geoffrey de Clinton	c. 1120 × 1129 1121 × 1123 1123 × 1126 1128–30	*RRAN*, II, nos. 1636, 1415, 1446; *PR 31 Henry I*, pp. 104–5.
? Roger	c. 1125	Witnessed charter of Nicholas son of Robert de Stafford for Kenilworth priory: BL Harley MS 3650, f. 26. Possibly under-sheriff.
? Ralph	c. 1125	Witnessed charter of Geoffrey I de Clinton for Kenilworth priory: BL Harley MS 3650, f. 2. Possibly under-sheriff.

<? William	c. 1150	*PRO Revised List*, p. 141, without source. Possibly William son of Corbucio: see above.>
? Hugh FitzRichard	before Mich 1155	Accounts *pro defectu Comitatus: PR 2–4 Henry II*, p. 87. If Hugh was being charged as a past sheriff, as is likely, then his tenure had come to an end by Mich 1155, when he was succeeded by Robert FitzHugh.

Wiltshire

Edric	1067	Mentioned as a landholder TRE: *DB*, I, 72b. *RRAN*, I, no. 9
Edward of Salisbury	occ. between 1070 and 1087	*RRAN*, I, nos. 135 (1081); II, 393–4 no. 136a (1081), 394 no. 137*; I, no. 149 (1082); see also no. 267 (1070 × 1087), addressed to Hugh de Port and Edward and Oda and Aegelsi and Saulf and Aelfsi at Haeccan and Cole and Eadric and all his thanes of Hampshire and Wiltshire.
	1086	*DB*, I, 64b, 69 where the identity of Edward with Edward of Salisbury is clear. For additional references as E. the sheriff: *RRAN*, I, nos. 194, 232, 247, 270, 283.
? O.	1078 × 1099	London, Westminster Abbey Muniment Book II, f. 679v, calendared *RRAN*, I, no. 417, printed *Westminster Abbey Charters*, no. 32, where it is suggested that the document was issued in William I's reign. It would appear that the scribe has mistakenly copied O. instead of E.
Walter	1087 × 1099 ? 1087	*RRAN*, II, 399. The gift of the manor of Bromham to Battle abbey is thought to have been made soon after William Rufus's accession: *Chron. Battle*, p. 96, says that the gift was made soon after his coronation. Hence it is not unreasonable to assume that this charter and *RRAN*, I, no. 290, were issued c. 1087. However, in terms of witnesses both could have been issued later. The limits of dating of the former are, on the one hand, the accession of William Rufus and, on the other, the death of Bishop Osmund of Salisbury. Walter the sheriff may have been either Walter Huse (see below) or Walter son of Edward of Salisbury, as the latter died not long after the Domesday Survey.
? Aiulf	1089 × 1091	Aiulf was sheriff of Dorset in 1086 and is described as Aiulf the sheriff in the *DB* account of Wiltshire: I, 73.
Walter Huse	1100 × 1110	*RRAN*, II, no. 673, and for other possible references, nos. 494, 593, 874, 883.
William de Pont de l'Arche	1110	*RRAN*, II, no. 948.
Walter son of Edward of Salisbury	1111 × 1114	*Cartulary of Winchester Cathedral*, no. 220, p. 100.
William	1113 × 1121, 1107 × 1122, 1113 × 1127 ? 1125–1128	*RRAN*, II, nos. 1185, 1291, 1517. *PR 31 Henry I*, p. 16. William left office by 1128 at the latest, yet his debt is so large that it must relate to several years' tenure. Presumably William de Pont de l'Arche, but note *PRO Revised List*, p. 152, for William son of Edward of Salisbury, 1115–1128 (without source).

Warin	from 1128 at the latest to 1130	*PR 31 Henry I*, p. 12;
	1128 × 1135	*RRAN*, II, no. 1937.
? Walter of Salisbury	1136 × 1140	Addressed (office not specified but concerns land which was in Wiltshire until late nineteenth century): *RRAN*, III, no. 684 and cf. II, no. 1862, a notification of Henry I concerning the same land and addressed to the sheriff of Wiltshire.
Earl Patrick	1153–1156	Accounts at Mich 1156 for farm of third year, i.e. 1153–1154 as well as following years: *PR 2–4 Henry II*, pp. 56–7; *RBE* II, 649. Note that there is a reference without source to a writ of Stephen in his 18th regnal year addressed to Earl Patrick as sheriff: *Complete Peerage*, XI, 136 n. (e) (not in *RRAN*, III).
Ralph Malet	1154–1155	Mentioned in account for Wiltshire but Earl Patrick renders the account so may have been under-sheriff: *RBE*, II, 649.
? Richard	occ. 1156	Pardoned danegeld in Wiltshire 1156: *PR 2–4 Henry II*, p. 59. Possibly Richard the clerk, sheriff of Wiltshire 1160–1162, but other possible identifications are Richard de Raddon, sheriff of Dorset 1154–1155, or Richard of Montacute, sheriff of Somerset for part of the same year.

Worcestershire

? Aevic	sheriff in reign of Cnut	Sheriff when Worcester cathedral's possession of Swinford (Staffs), Tardebigge and Clent (Worcs) was in dispute: *Hemingi Chartularium*, I, 277, 278. Not clear from context of which county he was sheriff.
Leofric	1017 × 1030	Harmer, no. 48 = S 991, possibly not authentic; cf. S 1423 (1016 × 1023): purchase by Evesham abbey of land at Norton (Worcs), and Robertson, no. 83 = S 1460 (1010 × 1023): recognition of bishop of Worcester's case over land at Inkberrow (Worcs); also comments by Williams, *Midland History*, XI (1986), 8.
Kineward	before 1086	As Kineward de Lauro witnessed grant of 1072. Described as sheriff in account of Bengeworth plea (1079 × 1083) but not necessarily sheriff at that time: *Hemingi Chartularium*, I, 80–3. Evidence discussed *Beauchamp Cart.*, p. xlviii.
Urse d'Abetot	probably by 1069 until death in 1108	In charge of building of Worcester castle before death of Archbishop Ealdred: WM, *Gesta Pontificum*, p. 253; *RRAN*, I, nos. 106 (1072 × 1077), 186 (1079 × 1083), 230 (1079 × 1086), 252 = *Cart. Worc.*, no. 2, p. 7, where dates of 1066 × 1080 are suggested, 429 (1100); II, nos. 488a, 501 (1100), 892 (1108); *DB*, I, 172, 175, 175b; *Cart. Worc.*, nos. 2 (1066 × 1080), 3 (1089). His death was recorded in the Winchcombe annals: Darlington, in *Medieval Miscellany for Doris Mary Stenton*, p. 122.
Roger d'Abetot	1108 × 1114	*Cart. Worc.*, nos. 41, pp. 26–7, as Roger (royal notification not in *RRAN*, II), 39 (1109 × 1111, 1113); *RRAN*, II, no. 940.
Osbert d'Abetot	1111 × 1115	*RRAN*, II, no. 1025.
Walter de Beauchamp	occ. between c. 1114 and c. 1133 d. by 1133	*RRAN*, II, no. 1034 (1114, cf. dating suggested in *Beauchamp Cart.*, no. 4, viz Dec 1113 × Apr 1116); see also nos. 1045 (1114 × 1118, cf. dating suggested in *Cart. Worc.*, no. 18, viz 1114 × 1118 or 1114 × 1131), 1386 (1109 × 1128, possibly 1123), 1887 (c. 1114 × 1133), 1710 (1130 × 1133). *RRAN*, II, no. 1710.
? Humphrey	occ. 1135 × 1139	Humphrey the sheriff of Wych (? Droitwich, Worcs) addressed in writ of Stephen for Gloucester abbey: *RRAN*, III, no. 356. Possibly reeve of Droitwich. See also under **Herefordshire**.

? Philip de Beaumais	1136 × 1140	*RRAN*, III, no. 966. Stephen addresses Waleran count of Meulan, Philip de Beaumais and all his ministers of Worcestershire and Staffordshire. Editor suggests Philip was apparently sheriff of Staffordshire, perhaps on grounds that William de Beauchamp may have been sheriff of Worcestershire.
William de Beauchamp	1139, 1141	Succeeded to father's office of dispenser by 1133 at latest, but no reference in king's charter to office of sheriff: *RRAN*, II, no. 1710.
	1139	Stephen granted him shrievalty: JW, p. 58;
	1141	Matilda granted him the office hereditarily: *RRAN*, III, no. 68. Died 1170: Worcester Annals, *Mon. Ang.*, IV, 382.
Payn	? before Mich 1154	*PR 2–4 Henry II*, p. 64, where referred to in past tense.
William Comin	1154–1155	*RBE*, II, 656.

Yorkshire[1]

? Gamel son of Osbern	1066 × 1069	Writ of King William addressed to Earl Morcar and Gamel son of Osbern: *Early Yorkshire Charters*, I, 86.
William Malet	1069	SD, II, 188; *DB*, I, 374.
Hugh FitzBaldric	1069 – c. 1080	SD, II, 201; *Early Yorkshire Charters*, I, 359; *DB*, I, 298, as Hugh the sheriff. Still living 1089, but apparently did not retain his English estates after the death of William the Conqueror: *Early Yorkshire Charters*, IX, xii, cf. 70–6.
Erneis de Buron	before 1086	*RRAN*, I, 403 (dated by editor 1070 × 1098, but see comments in *Early Yorkshire Charters*, III, 123). *RRAN*, I, no. 226 (1070 × 1086).
Ralph Paynel	1088	SD, I, 172–3.
Geoffrey Bainard	overall limits of dating 1070 × 1100, but c. 1089 – c. 1095	*RRAN*, I, nos. 421 (1087 × 1099) as G. the sheriff, 344 (1087 × 1099, but B & C, no. 8, suggest 1089 × 1091) as Geoffrey Bainard but without specifying office and 431 (1070 × 1100) also without specifying office.
H.	1096 × 1100	*RRAN*, I, no. 480 and see also no. 412 = B & C, no. 11 (1097 × 1098).
? Bertram de Verdon	1100, Jan or Feb to ? 20 Sept	*RRAN*, I, no. 427 (office not specified); II, no. 495 (office not specified), and see note there amending date of *RRAN*, I, no. 427.
? Robert de Lacy	occ. between 1100 and 1118	*RRAN*, II, nos. 496 (1100 × 1107), 559 (1101, or 1104 × 1108), 561 (1102), 598 (1102). If Robert occurs other than as a local magnate, it is perhaps as local justiciar, since Osbert seems to have been sheriff from 1100. See also *RRAN*, II, no. 1030 (1108 × 1114), addressed to the archbishop of York, Robert de Lacy, Nigel d'Aubigny and all the barons of Yorkshire and Nottinghamshire.
Osbert the sheriff	25 Dec 1100 – c. 1115	*RRAN*, II, nos. 505 (25 Dec 1100), 546 (1101 × 1107), 590 (1102), 648 (1103), 669 (1103 × 1104), 681 (1101 × 1114), 704–5 (1105), 714 (1103 × 1105, concerns Yorkshire), 748 (1103 × 1106), 796 (1106), 799 (1101 × 1104), 836 (1100 × 1107), 837 (1101 × 1107), 838 (1100 × 1113), 839 (1102, 1103, 1105, 1107), 852 (1103 × 1107), 891 (1100 or 1108 × 1114), 917 (1108 × 1114), 926–7 (1108 × 1114), 977 (1108 × 1114), 995 (1109 × 1114), 1046 (1100 × 1115, concerns Yorkshire), 1112 (1100 × 1113 as O.), 1113 (1106 × 1115), and for other possible references see index to *RRAN*, II.

1. See also W. Farrer, *EHR*, XXX (1915), 277–85.

Anschetil of Bulmer	1114 × 1129,	*RRAN*, II, nos. 1072,
	1120 × 1122,	1286,
	1122,	1336,
	1115 × 1129	1621, and for other possible references see index to *RRAN*, II. Living 1127, when attended consecration of Robert, bishop of St Andrews: *Early Scottish Charters*, no. lxxvi pp. 64–5; for date see: Nicholl, *Thurstan, Archbishop of York*, p. 102.
Bertram of Bulmer	1128–1130	*PR 31 Henry I*, p. 24.
	1155, Jan–Mich	*RBE*, II, 652.
Robert of Octon	before 1154	Sheriff of Yorkshire before becoming monk at Meaux abbey. Succeeded in lands by son Henry before 1160: *Chron. Melsa*, I, 102.
? William	c. 1150	Attests fine between William, count of Aumale and John of Meaux: *Early Yorkshire Charters*, III, 90.
? Ralph the sheriff	? 1144 × 1154	Witnesses *Charters of the Honour of Mowbray*, nos. 100 (c. 1144 × May 1155), 105 (c. 1144 × Nov 1156), 204 (c. 1154 × 1175), pp. 74, 77–8, 144–5. Possibly sheriff of Richmond rather than Yorkshire. Ralph the sheriff received land from the earl of Richmond; this man may have been Ralph the sheriff of Ainderby who occurs at a slightly later date and may have been sheriff of Richmond: *Early Yorkshire Charters*, IV, 138–9, 115–17, 241, 357.

Bibliography

Manuscript sources

Cambridge University Library Additional MSS 3020, 3021
Durham, Dean and Chapter Muniments
  Almoner's Small Cartulary
  4. 3. Ebor. 4
  3. 1. Pont. 18
London, British Library
  Additional Charters 19588, 65175
  Additional MS 40008
  Cotton MSS:
    Cleopatra C VII
    Domitian A X
    Faustina A III
    Otho D III
    Vespasian A XVIII
    Vespasian B XXIV
  Harley MSS 3650, 4757
  Royal 11 B IX
London, Lambeth Palace, Christ Church Canterbury
  Register A
London, Lincoln's Inn MS 87
London, Public Record Office
  Chancery Masters' Exhibits: Duchess of Norfolk
    Deeds: C 115/K1/6679
  Record Commission Transcripts: Series II:
    Cartulaire de la Basse Normandie:
    PRO 31/8/140B
London, Westminster Abbey Muniment Book II
Maidstone, Kent County Record Office, DRc/T373
Oxford, Balliol College, MS 271
Oxford, Bodleian Library, MS Top. Yorks. e. 9
San Marino, California, U.S.A., Huntington Library
  BA 42/1132, 42/1150, 14/1526, 14/1530
Wells, Dean and Chapter, Liber Albus

Printed primary sources

The Acta of the Bishops of Chichester, 1075–1207, ed. H. Mayr-Harting (Canterbury and York Society, LVI, 1964).
Anglo-Saxon Charters, ed. A.J. Robertson (Cambridge, 1939).
The Anglo-Saxon Chronicle: a revised translation, ed. D. Whitelock, D.C. Douglas and S.I. Tucker (London, 1961).

Annales Cambriae, ed. J. Williams ab Ithel (Rolls Series, London, 1860).
The Beauchamp Cartulary Charters 1100–1268, ed. E. Mason (Pipe Roll Society, new series, XLIII, 1980 for 1971–3).
Book of Fees: Liber Feodorum. The Book of Fees commonly called Testa de Nevill, reformed from the earliest MSS by the Deputy Keeper of the Records (London, 1920–31).
Calendar of Documents preserved in France, illustrative of the History of Great Britain and Ireland, I, *A.D. 918–1216*, ed. J.H. Round (London, 1899).
Calendar of the Manuscripts of the Dean and Chapter of Wells, I (Historical Manuscripts Commission, London, 1907).
The Carmen de Hastingae Proelio of Guy Bishop of Amiens, ed. C. Morton and H. Muntz (Oxford, 1972).
The Cartae Antiquae Rolls 11–20, ed. L. Landon (Pipe Roll Society, new series, XXXII, 1957).
Cartularium de Colecestria, ed. S.A. Moore (2 vols., Roxburghe Club, 1897).
Cartularium Monasterii de Ramesia, ed. W.H. Hart and P.A. Lyons (3 vols., Rolls Series, London, 1884–93).
Cartularium Prioratus de Colne, ed. E.J. Fisher (Essex Archaeological Society Occasional Publications, I, 1946).
The Cartulary of Boxgrove Priory, ed. L. Fleming (Sussex Record Society, LIX, 1960).
Cartulary of Holy Trinity Aldgate, ed. G.A.J. Hodgett (London Record Society, VII, 1971).
The Cartulary of Launceston Priory, ed. P.L. Hull (Devon and Cornwall Record Society, new series, XXX, 1987).
The Cartulary of Missenden Abbey, ed. J.G. Jenkins (2 vols., Buckinghamshire Record Society, II, X, 1939 for 1938, 1955).
Cartulary of the Monastery of St Frideswide, ed. S.R. Wigram (2 vols., Oxfordshire Historical Society, XXVIII, XXXI, 1895–6).
Cartulary of Oseney Abbey, ed. H.E. Salter, (6 vols., Oxford Historical Society, LXXXIX–XCI, XCVII–XCVIII, CI, 1929–1936).
The Cartulary of Shrewsbury Abbey, ed. U. Rees (2 vols., Aberystwyth, 1975).
The Cartulary of Worcester Cathedral Priory, ed. R.R. Darlington (Pipe Roll Society, LXXVI, 1968 for 1962–3).

Charters and Documents illustrating the History of the Cathedral, City and Diocese of Salisbury in the Twelfth and Thirteenth Centuries, selected by W. Rich Jones and ed. W. Dunn Macray (Rolls Series, London, 1891).

Charters of the Anglo-Norman Earls of Chester c. 1071–1237, ed. G. Barraclough (Lancashire and Cheshire Record Society, CXXVI, 1988).

Charters of the Earldom of Hereford, ed. D. Walker, Camden Miscellany, XXII (Camden Society, 4th series, I, 1964), 1–75.

Charters of the Honour of Mowbray 1107–1191, ed. D.E. Greenway (British Academy, Records of Social and Economic History, new series, I, London, 1972).

Charters of Rochester, ed. A. Campbell, Anglo-Saxon Charters I (London, 1973).

The Chartulary of the Priory of St Pancras of Lewes, ed. L.F. Salzman (2 vols., Sussex Record Society, XXXVIII, XL, 1933–5).

Chartulary of the Priory of St Peter at Sele, ed. L.F. Salzman (Cambridge, 1923).

Chartulary of Winchester Cathedral, calendared A.W. Goodman (Winchester, 1927).

The Chartulary or Register of the Abbey of St Werburgh Chester, ed. J. Tait (2 vols., Chetham Society, LXXIX, LXXXII, 1920, 1923).

Chronica Monasterii de Melsa, ed. E.A. Bond (3 vols., Rolls Series, London, 1866–8).

The Chronicle of Battle Abbey, ed. and trans. E. Searle (Oxford, 1980).

The Chronicle of John of Worcester, ed. J.R.H. Weaver, (Anecdota Oxoniensia, mediaeval and modern series, XII, Oxford, 1908).

Chronicon Abbatiae Rameseiensis, ed. W. Dunn Macray (Rolls Series, London, 1886).

Chronicon Cumbrie in The Register of the Priory of St Bees, ed. J. Wilson (Surtees Society, CXXVI, 1915), 491–6.

Chronicon Monasterii de Abingdon, ed. J. Stevenson (2 vols., Rolls Series, London, 1858).

Councils and Synods with other Documents relating to the English Church, I (2), 1066–1204, ed. D. Whitelock, M. Brett and C.N.L. Brooke (Oxford, 1981).

Dialogus de Scaccario, ed. and trans. C. Johnson with corrections by F.E.L. Carter and D.E. Greenway (Oxford, 1983).

Documents of the Baronial Movement of Reform and Rebellion 1258–1267, selected R.F. Treharne, ed. I.J. Sanders (Oxford, 1973).

Domesday Book: Dorset, ed. C. Thorn and F. Thorn (Phillimore, Chichester, 1983).

Domesday Book seu Liber Censualis Willelmi Primi Regis Angliae, I, II, ed. A. Farley, III, IV, ed. H. Ellis (4 vols., Record Commission, London 1783–1816). References are to this edition unless otherwise stated.

The Domesday Monachorum of Christ Church, Canterbury, ed. D.C. Douglas (London, 1944).

Dugdale, W. Monasticon Anglicanum (new edn, 6 vols. in 8, London, 1817–30).

Durham Episcopal Charters, ed. H.S. Offler (Surtees Society, CLXXIX, 1968).

Early Scottish Charters prior to A.D. 1153, ed. A.C. Lawrie (Cambridge, 1905).

Early Yorkshire Charters, I–III, ed. W. Farrer (Edinburgh, 1914–16); IV–XII, ed. C.T. Clay (Yorkshire Archaeological Society, record series, extra series, I–III, V–X, 1935–65).

English Episcopal Acta, I, Lincoln 1067–1185, ed. D.M. Smith (London, 1980).

English Historical Documents, I, ed. D. Whitelock (2nd edn, London, 1979); II, 1042–1189 ed. D.C. Douglas and G.W. Greenaway (2nd edn, London, 1981).

Eynsham Cartulary, ed. H.E. Salter (2 vols., Oxford Historical Society, XLIX, LI, 1907–8).

Facsimiles of Early Charters preserved in Oxford Muniment Rooms, ed. H.E. Salter (Oxford, 1929).

Facsimiles of English Royal Writs to A.D. 1100 presented to V.H. Galbraith, ed. T.A.M. Bishop and P. Chaplais (Oxford, 1957).

Feudal Documents from the Abbey of Bury St Edmunds, ed. D.C. Douglas (British Academy, Records of the Social and Economic History of England and Wales, London, 1932).

The First Register of Norwich Cathedral Priory, ed. H.W. Saunders (Norfolk Record Society, XI, 1939).

Florence of Worcester, Chronicon ex Chronicis, ed. B. Thorpe (2 vols., London, 1848, 1849).

Frithegodi Monachi Breuiloquium Vitae Beati Wilfredi et Wulfstani Cantoris Narratio Metrica de Sancto Swithuno, ed. A. Campbell (Zurich, 1950).

Gesta Stephani, ed. and trans. K.R. Potter, 2nd edn with new introduction and notes by R.H.C. Davis (Oxford, 1976).

Gervase of Canterbury, The Historical Works, ed. W. Stubbs (2 vols., Rolls Series, London, 1879–80).

The Great Register of Lichfield Cathedral, known as Magnum Registrum Album, ed. H.E. Savage (William Salt Archaeological Society, third series, 1926 for 1924).

Hemingi Chartularium Ecclesiae Wigorniensis, ed. T. Hearne (2 vols., Oxford, 1723).

Herefordshire Domesday, ed. V.H. Galbraith and J. Tait (Pipe Roll Society, new series, XXV, 1950 for 1947–8).

Historia et Cartularium Monasterii Sancti Petri Gloucestriae, ed. W. Hart (3 vols., Rolls Series, London, 1863–7).

Inquisitio Comitatus Cantabrigiensis, ed. N.E.S.A. Hamilton (London, 1876).

John of Hexham, *Historia*, in Symeon of Durham, *Opera Omnia*, ed. T. Arnold, (2 vols., Rolls Series, London, 1882–5).

John of Oxenedes, *Chronica*, ed. H. Ellis (Rolls Series, London, 1859).

Leges Henrici Primi, ed. and trans. L.J. Downer (Oxford, 1972).

The Letters and Charters of Gilbert Foliot, ed. A. Morey and C.N.L. Brooke (Cambridge, 1967).

The Letters of John of Salisbury, vol. I. *The Early Letters (1153–1161)*, ed. W.J. Millor, S.J. and H.E. Butler, revised by C.N.L. Brooke (Edinburgh, 1955).

Liber Eliensis, ed. E.O. Blake, Camden Society, 3rd Series, XCII (1962).

Liber Memorandum de Bernewelle, ed. J.W. Clark (Cambridge, 1907).

The Life of St William of Norwich, ed. A. Jessopp and M.R. James (Cambridge, 1896).

The Lincolnshire Domesday and the Lindsey Survey, ed. C.W. Foster and T. Longley (Lincoln Record Society, XIX, 1921).

Materials for the History of Thomas Becket, archbishop of Canterbury canonized by Pope Alexander III, A.D. 1173, I–VI, ed. J.C. Robertson, VII, ed. J.C. Robertson and J.B. Sheppard (7 vols., Rolls Series, London, 1875–85).

Matthew Paris, *Chronica Majora*, ed. H.R. Luard (7 vols., Rolls Series, London, 1872–3).

Memorials of St. Edmund's Abbey, ed. T. Arnold (3 vols., Rolls Series, London, 1890–96).

Orderic Vitalis, *The Ecclesiastical History*, ed. M. Chibnall (6 vols., Oxford, 1969–80).

Pipe Rolls:

The Great Rolls of the Pipe for the Second, Third and Fourth Years of the Reign of King Henry the Second, 1155–1158, ed. J. Hunter (Record Commission, London, 1844).

The Great Roll of the Pipe for the Sixth Year of the Reign of King Henry the Second (Pipe Roll Society, II, 1884).

The Great Roll of the Pipe for the Seventh Year of the Reign of King Henry the Second (Pipe Roll Society, IV, 1885).

Magnum Rotuli Scaccarii vel Magnum Rotulum Pipae de Anno Tricesimo-primo Regni Henrici Primi, ed. J. Hunter (Record Commission, London, 1833).

Radulfi de Diceto Decani Lundoniensis Opera Historica, ed. W. Stubbs (2 vols., Rolls Series, London, 1876).

Reading Abbey Cartularies, ed. B.R. Kemp (Camden Society, 4th series, XXXI, XXXIII, 1986, 1987).

The Records of Merton Priory, ed. A. Heales (London, 1898).

The Red Book of the Exchequer, ed. H. Hall (3 vols., Rolls Series, London, 1896).

Regesta Regum Anglo-Normannorum 1066–1154, I, ed. H.W.C. Davis, II, ed. C. Johnson and H.A. Cronne, III and IV, ed. H.A. Cronne and R.H.C. Davis (4 vols., Oxford, 1913–69).

Regesta Regum Scottorum, I, *Malcolm IV 1153–1165*, ed. G.W.S. Barrow (Edinburgh, 1960).

The Register of the Priory of St Bees, ed. J. Wilson (Surtees Society, CXXVI, 1915).

Registrum Antiquissimum of the Cathedral Church of Lincoln, ed. C.W. Foster and K. Major (10 vols., Lincoln Record Society, 1931–68).

St Benet of Holme 1020–1210, ed. J.R. West (Norfolk Record Society, II, III (1932).

Select Charters, ed. W. Stubbs, 9th edn, revised by H.W.C. Davis (Oxford, 1913).

Sibton Abbey Cartularies and Charters, ed. P. Brown in *Suffolk Charters*, VII, VIII, IX (Suffolk Record Society, 1985–7).

Sir Christopher Hatton's Book of Seals, ed. L.C. Loyd and D.M. Stenton (Northamptonshire Record Society, XV, 1950).

Symeon of Durham, *Opera Omnia*, ed. T. Arnold, (2 vols., Rolls Series, London, 1882–5).

Textus Roffensis, ed. P. Sawyer (Early English Manuscripts in Facsimile, VII, IX, Copenhagen, 1957, 1962).

Two Cartularies of the Augustinian Priory of Bruton and the Cluniac Priory of Montacute (Somerset Record Society, VIII, 1894).

Westminster Abbey Charters c. 1066–1214, ed. E. Mason, assisted by J. Bray (London Record Society, XXV, 1988).

William of Malmesbury *De Gestis Pontificum Anglorum Libri Quinque*, ed. N.E.S.A. Hamilton (Rolls Series, London, 1870).

William of Poitiers, *Gesta Guillelmi*, ed. R. Foreville (Paris, 1952).

Winton Domesday in *Winchester in the Early Middle Ages*, ed. M. Biddle (Winchester Studies, I, Oxford, 1976).

Secondary sources

Adams, C. Phythian, 'Rutland reconsidered', in *Mercian Studies*, ed. A. Dornier (Leicester, 1977), pp. 63–84.

Barlow, F., *William Rufus* (London, 1983).

Barrow, G.W.S., 'King David I and the Honour of Lancaster', *EHR*, LXX (1955), 85–9.

'The charters of Henry I', *Scottish Historical Review*, XXXVI (1957), 59–62.

The Anglo-Norman Era in Scottish History (Oxford, 1980).

Bird, W.H., 'Osbert the Sheriff', *Genealogist*, new series, XXXII (1916), 1–6, 73–83, 153–60, 227–32.

Blair, C.H. Hunter, 'The sheriffs of Northumberland', *Archaeologia Aeliana*, 4th series, XX (1942), 11–91.

'The sheriffs of the County of Durham', *Archaeologia Aeliana*, 4th series, XXII (1944), 22–82.

Bouvris, J.-M., 'Contribution à une étude de l'institution vicomtale en Normandie au XIe siècle. L'example de la partie orientale du duché: les vicomtes de Rouen et de Fécamp', in L. Musset, J.-M. Bouvris, J.-M. Maillefer, *Autour du pouvoir ducal normand x^e – xiie siècles*. Cahier des *Annales de Normandie*, no. 17 (Caen, 1985), pp. 149–74.

Brooke, C.N.L. and Keir, G., *London 800–1216: The Shaping of a City* (London, 1975).

Brooke, C.N.L., Keir, G., Reynolds, S., 'Henry I's charter for London', *Journal of the Society of Archivists*, IV (1970–4), 558–78.

Caenegem, R.C. van, *Royal Writs in England from the Conquest to Glanvill* (Selden Society, LXXVII, 1959 for 1958–9).

Cam, H., 'Manerium cum hundredo: The hundred and the hundredal manor', *EHR*, XLVII (1932), 353–76; reprinted in *Liberties and Communities in Medieval England* (Cambridge, 1944), pp. 64–90.

'An East Anglian shire-moot of Stephen's reign, 1148–53', *EHR*, XXXIX (1924), 568–71.

Campbell, J., 'Some agents and agencies of the late Anglo-Saxon state' in *Domesday Studies: Papers Read at the Novocentenary Conference of the Royal Historical Society and the Institute of British Geographers Winchester, 1986*, ed. J.C. Holt (Woodbridge, 1987), pp. 201–18.

Carpenter, D., 'The decline of the curial sheriff in England 1194–1258', *EHR*, XCI (1976), 1–32.

Clanchy, M.T., *From Memory to Written Record* (London, 1979).

Colker, M.L., 'Latin texts concerning Gilbert, founder of Merton priory', *Studia Monastica*, XII (1970), 241–71.

Complete Peerage, by G.E.C., revised edn, V. Gibbs, H.A. Doubleday, G.H. White (13 vols. in 12, London, 1910–59).

Cronne, H.A., 'The Honour of Lancaster in Stephen's reign', *EHR*, L (1935), 670–80.

'The office of local justiciar in England under the Norman kings', *University of Birmingham Historical Journal*, VI (1957–8), 18–28.

Crook, D., 'The establishment of the Derbyshire County Court, 1256', *Derbyshire Archaeological Journal*, CIII (1983), 98–106.

Crouch, D., 'Geoffrey de Clinton and Roger Earl of Warwick: new men and magnates in the reign of Henry I', *Bulletin of the Institute of Historical Research*, LV (1982), 113–24.

The Beaumont Twins: The Roots and Branches of Power in the Twelfth Century, (Cambridge Studies in Medieval Life and Thought, 4th series, I, Cambridge, 1986).

Darlington, R.R., 'Winchcombe Annals 1049–1181', in *A Medieval Miscellany for Doris Mary Stenton* (Pipe Roll Society, new series, XXXV, 1962 for 1960).

Davis, R.H.C., *King Stephen* (London, 1967).

'The College of St Martin-le-Grand and the Anarchy, 1135–1154', *London Topographical Record*, XXIII (1974 for 1972), 9–26.

Deputy Keeper of the Public Records, Thirty-first Report (London, 1870).

Deputy Keeper of the Public Records, Thirty-fifth Report (London, 1874).

Douglas, D.C., *William the Conqueror* (London, 1964).

Eyton, R.W., *Antiquities of Shropshire* (12 vols., London and Shifnal, 1854–60).

'Robert FitzWymarch and his descendants', *Shropshire Archaeological and Natural History Society*, II (1879), 1–34.

Farrer, W., 'The sheriffs of Lincolnshire and Yorkshire, 1066–1130', *EHR*, XXX (1915), 277–85.

An Outline Itinerary of Henry I, first published *EHR*, XXXIV (1919); references are to the reprinted edn (Oxford, 1919).

Honors and Knights' Fees (3 vols., London and Manchester, 1923–5).

Fowler, G.H., 'Some Saxon charters', *Publications of the Bedfordshire Historical Record Society*, V (1920), 39–57.

Freeman, E.A., *The History of the Norman Conquest*, (5 vols. and index, Oxford, 1870–9).

Gray, A., *The Priory of St Radegund* (Cambridge, 1898).

Green, J.A., 'The last century of danegeld', *EHR*, XCVI (1981), 241–58.

'The sheriffs of William the Conqueror' in *Anglo-Norman Studies: Proceedings of the Battle Conference on Anglo-Norman Studies 1982*, V (1983), 129–45.

The Government of England under Henry I (Cambridge Studies in Medieval Life and Thought, 4th series, III, Cambridge, 1986).

'Ranulf II and Lancashire', conference paper delivered at Chester in July 1988, to be published by the *Chester Archaeological Society*.

Harmer, F.E. *Anglo-Saxon Writs* (Manchester, 1952).

Haskins, C.H., *Norman Institutions* (Cambridge, Mass., 1918).

The Heads of Religious Houses England and Wales 940–1216, ed. D. Knowles, C.N.L. Brooke and V. London (Cambridge, 1972).

Hedley, W. Percy, *Northumberland Families* (2 vols., Newcastle upon Tyne, 1968, 1970).

Hollister, C. Warren, *Anglo-Saxon Military Institutions* (Oxford, 1962).

Holt, J.C., *The Northerners* (Oxford, 1961).

Jolliffe, J.E.A., *The Constitutional History of Medieval England* (London, 1937).

John, E., 'English feudalism and the structure of Anglo-Saxon society', *Bulletin of the John Rylands Library*, XLVI (1962), 14–41.

Kapelle, W.E., *The Norman Conquest of the North* (London, 1979).

Kealey, E.J., *Roger of Salisbury* (Berkeley, Los Angeles and London, 1972).

Kellaway, W., 'The coroner in medieval London' in *Studies in London History presented to Philip Edmund Jones*, ed. A.E.J. Hollaender and W. Kellaway (London, 1969), 75–91.

Keynes, S., *The Diplomas of King Aethelred 'the Unready' 978–1016*, (Cambridge Studies in Medieval Life and Thought, 3rd series, XIII, Cambridge, 1980).

Landon, L., 'The sheriffs of Norfolk', *Norfolk Archaeology*, XXIII (1929), 147–64.

Latimer, P., 'Grants of "totus comitatus" in twelfth-century England: their origins and meaning', *Bulletin of the Institute of Historical Research*, LIX (1986), 137–45.

Le Neve, J., *Fasti Ecclesiae Anglicanae 1066–1300*, compiled by D.E. Greenway, I, *St Paul's Cathedral* (London, 1968).

Lewis, C., 'The Norman settlement of Herefordshire under William I' in *Anglo-Norman Studies. Proceedings of the Battle Conference on Anglo-Norman Studies 1984*, VII (1985), 195–213.

Lieberman, F., *Ungedruckte Anglo-normannische Geschichtsquellen* (Strassburg, 1879).

List of Sheriffs for England and Wales from the earliest Times to A.D. 1831 compiled from documents in the Public Record Office. Lists and Indexes IX, Public Record Office (originally published London, 1898; reprinted with amendments by M. Mills, New York, 1963).

Loyd, L.C., *The Origins of Some Anglo-Norman Families*, (Harleian Society, CIII, Leeds, 1951).

Loyn, H.R., 'The hundred in England in the tenth and early eleventh century' in *British Government and Administration: Studies presented to S.B. Chrimes*, ed. H. Hearder and H.R. Loyn (Cardiff, 1974), pp. 1–15.

The Governance of Anglo-Saxon England 500–1087. The Governance of England, I (London, 1984).

Mack, K., 'The stallers: administrative innovation in the reign of Edward the Confessor', *Journal of Medieval History*, XII (1986), 123–35.

Mahany C. and Roffe, D., 'Stamford: the development of an Anglo-Scandinavian borough' in *Anglo-Norman Studies. Proceedings of the Battle Conference on Anglo-Norman Studies 1982*, V (1983), 197–219.

Major, K., 'Blyborough Charters', in *A Medieval Miscellany for Doris Mary Stenton*, ed. P.M. Barnes and C.F. Slade (Pipe Roll Society, new series, XXXV, 1962 for 1960).

Mason, E., 'The King, the Chamberlain, and Southwick Priory', *Bulletin of the Institute of Historical Research*, LIII (1980), 1–10.

Mason, J.F.A., 'The officers and clerks of the Norman earls of Shropshire' *Transactions of the Shropshire Archaeological Society*, LVI (1957–60), 244–57.

'Roger de Montgomery and his sons (1067–1102)', *Transactions of the Royal Historical Society*, 5th series, XIII (1963), 1–28.

'William I and the Sussex Rapes' (Historical Association, Hastings and Bexhill Branch, 1966).

Morris, W.A., *The Frankpledge System* (London, 1910). *The Medieval English Sheriff to 1300* (Manchester, 1927).

Nicholl, D., *Thurstan Archbishop of York 1114–40* (York, 1964).

Ormerod, G., *History of Cheshire*, 2nd edn by T. Helsby (3 vols., London, 1882).

Padel, O., 'Geoffrey of Monmouth and Cornwall', *Cambridge Medieval Celtic Studies*, VIII (1984), 1–27.

Prestwich, J.O., 'The military household of the Norman kings', *EHR*, XCVI (1981), 1–35.

'The treason of Geoffrey de Mandeville', with an appendix by R.H.C. Davis, *EHR*, CIII (1988), 283–317.

Reynolds, S., 'The rulers of London in the twelfth

century', *History*, LVII, (1972), 337–57.

Robinson, J. Armitage, *Gilbert Crispin* (Cambridge, 1911).

Roffe, D., 'The Lincolnshire hundred', *Landscape History*, III (1982), 27–36.

'The origins of Derbyshire', *Derbyshire Archaeological Journal*, CVI (1986), 102–22.

Round, J.H., *Geoffrey de Mandeville* (London, 1892).

'Odard of Carlisle', *Genealogist*, VIII (1892), 200–4.

Feudal England (London, 1895). References are to the reset edn of 1964.

The Commune of London (London, 1899).

'The early sheriffs of Norfolk', *EHR*, XXXV (1920), 481–96.

Royal Commission on Historical Manuscripts. Third Report (London, 1872).

Royal Commission on Historical Manuscripts. Eighth Report (London, 1881).

Royal Commission on Historical Manuscripts. Ninth Report (London, 1883).

Saltman, A., *Theobald Archbishop of Canterbury* (London, 1956).

Sanders, I.J., *Feudal Baronies* (Oxford, 1960).

Sawyer, P.H., *Anglo-Saxon Charters: an Annotated List and Bibliography*, (Royal Historical Society, London, 1968).

Stafford, P., 'The reign of Aethelred II, a study in the limitations on royal policy and actions', *Ethelred the Unready: Papers from the Millenary Conference* ed. D. Hill (British Archaeological Reports, British series LIX, 1978), 15–46.

'The "farm of one night" and the organization of King Edward's estates in Domesday', *Economic History Review*, 2nd series, XXXIII (1980), 491–502.

Stenton, D.M., *English Justice between the Norman Conquest and the Great Charter, 1066–1215* (London, 1965).

Stenton, F.M., 'St Benet of Holme and the Norman Conquest', *EHR*, XXXVII (1922), 225–35.

The First Century of English Feudalism 1066–1166 (2nd edn, Oxford, 1971).

Anglo-Saxon England, 3rd edn (Oxford, 1971).

Tait, J., *Mediaeval Manchester and the Beginnings of Lancashire* (Manchester, 1904).

Taylor, C.S., 'The origins of the Mercian shires' in *Gloucestershire Studies*, ed. H.P.R. Finberg (Leicester, 1957), pp. 17–51.

Walker, Curtis H., 'Sheriffs in the pipe roll of 31 Henry I', *EHR*, XXXVII (1922), 67–79.

'The date of the Conqueror's ordinance separating the ecclesiastical and lay courts', *English Historical Review*, XXXIX (1924), 399–400.

Walker, D., 'Miles of Gloucester, earl of Hereford', *Transactions of the Bristol and Gloucestershire Archaeological Society*, LXXVII (1958), 66–96.

Wedgwood, J.C., 'Staffordshire sheriffs, 1086–1912, escheators, 1247–1619, and keepers or justices of the peace 1263–1702', *William Salt Archaeological Society*, 3rd Series, (1912), 272–344.

Whitelock, D. *Anglo-Saxon Wills* (Cambridge, 1930).

'The dealings of the kings of England with Northumbria in the tenth and eleventh centuries', in *The Anglo-Saxons: Studies presented to Bruce Dickins* (London, 1959), pp. 70–88.

Wightman, W.E., *The Lacy Family in England and Normandy 1066–1194* (Oxford, 1966).

Williams, A., '"Cockles amongst the wheat"; Danes and English in the Western Midlands in the first half of the eleventh century', *Midland History*, XI (1986), 1–22.

Young, A., *William Cumin: Border Politics and the Bishopric of Durham 1141–1144* (Borthwick Papers, no. 54, Borthwick Institute of Historical Research, York, n.d.).

Unpublished theses

Amt, E.M., 'From Tempus Werre to Pax Publica: the Reconstruction of Royal Government in England c. 1149–c. 1159' (Oxford D.Phil. thesis, 1988).

Bearman, R., 'Charters of the Redvers Family and the Earldom of Devon in the Twelfth Century' (London Ph.D. thesis, 1981).

White, G., 'The Restoration of Order in England 1153–4', (Cambridge Ph.D. thesis, 1974).

Index of Persons and Places

's.' denotes 'sheriff'

Abetot, Osbert d', s. Worcs, 87
  Roger d', s. Worcs, 87
  Urse d', s. Worcs, 13, 16, 17, 87
Abingdon, Berks, abbey, 26, 40, 57
  abbot of *see* Faritius
Adam, ? s. or under-s. Berks, 27
Adam, s. Sussex, rape of Lewes, 82
Adeliza, queen of England, widow of Henry I, later wife
    of William d'Aubigny, 80
Adelulf, ? s. Sussex, rape of Pevensey, 82
Aegelsi, 85
Aelfgaet, s. London/Midd, 56
Aelfgar the king's reeve, 22 n. 111
Aelfnoth, s. Heref, 11, 45
Aelfsi, 85
Aelfstan, s. Beds, 25
Aelfwig *see* Aluui, Alwi
Aethelith, 25
Aethelnoth, governor (*satrapa*) of Canterbury, ? s. Kent,
    50
Aethelred, king of England, 9, 10, 22 n. 111
Aethelric, 22 n. 113
Aethelwine, shireman/s. Kent, 22 n. 113, 50
Aethelwine *see* Aluuin
Aevic, ? s. Staffs or Worcs, 17, 75, 87
Aigle, Gilbert de l', 80
  Richer de l', 80
Ailsi, abbot of Ramsey, 48
Ailwin, ? s. Sussex, 80
Ailwy, ? s. Norf, 60
Ainderby, Ralph of, ? s. Richmond, Yorks, 90
Aiulf, 19, 23 n. 119; ? s. Berks, 26; s. Dorset, 37;
    s. Som, 73; ? s. Wilts, 85
Alan, count [of Brittany], 60
Alan, ? s. or under-s. Heref, 43
Aldwin, abbot of Ramsey, 61
Aldwin, chamberlain of Queen Matilda, first wife of
    Henry I, ? s. Essex, 40
Alfred, ? s. Berks or Essex, 26, 40
Alfred, s. Dorset, 37
Alured, ? s. or under-s. Essex, 40
Aluric, s. Hunts, 48
Aluui (Aelfwig), ? s. Glos or Oxon, 42, 69
Aluuin (Aethelwine), ? s. Glos, Heref, Hunts or Warw,
    42, 45, 48, 83
  son of *see* Warwick, Turchil of

Alwi (Aelfwig), ? s. Glos or Oxon, 42, 69
Amfrid, ? *alias* Anfrid *collector*, ? s. Essex, 40
Anjou, count of, heir of, 14
Anselm, abbot of Bury St Edmunds, 61
Anselm, *vicomte* of Rouen, s. Berks, 27
Ansfrid, s. Kent, 17, 20 n. 49, 51
Ansger the staller, 15, 20 n. 32, 22 n. 113
Archenfield, Heref, 45
Arthur, s. Salop, 71
Arundel, Sussex, rape of, sheriffs of, 80, 81
Aubigny, Nigel d', 89
  William d', 80
    Adeliza wife of *see* Adeliza, queen of England
Aumale, count of *see* William
Avranches, Normandy, *vicomte* of, *see* 'Radulphus'
Avranches, Hugh d', earl of Chester, 12
Avranches, Rualon d', ? s. Kent, 16, 50
Azor, s. Oxon, 70

Bacon, William, s. Beds, 25
Bailleul, Renaud de, s. Salop, 71, 72
  Amieria wife of, niece of Roger of Montgomery, earl
      of Shrewsbury, and widow of Warin, 71
Bainard, Geoffrey, s. Yorks, 89
  Ralph, castellan of Baynard's castle, ? s. London/
      Midd, 56
  William, castellan of Baynard's castle, ? s. London/
      Midd, 56
Baldric, Hugh son of, *alias* Hugh FitzBaldric,
    ? s. Lincs, 54; s. Notts, 67; s. Yorks, 89
Baldwin, ? s. Corn, 33; ? s. Devon, 35
  Richard son of, s. Corn, 33; s. Devon, 22 n. 89, 35,
      36; s. Som, 73
    Adelicia sister of, and Matilda her daughter, 35
  Robert son of, 35
  William son of, ? s. Devon, 35
Balio, William de, s. London/Midd, 58
Bamburgh, Odard of, s. Northumb, 31, 65
  Adam son of, 65
Bardney, Lincs, abbey, 55
Barnwell, Cambs, priory, 29
Basset, Ralph, 26
  Richard, 14, 16, 75; s. Beds, 25; s. Bucks, 28;
      s. Cambs, 29; s. Essex, 40; s. Herts, 47;
      s. Hunts, 48; s. Leics, 53; s. Norf, 61;
      s. Northants, 64; s. Suff, 77; s. Surrey, 78
Bath, bishop of *see* John
Bath, Rayner of, s. Lincs, 55

Battle, Sussex, abbey, 80, 85
Bayeux, Normandy, bishop of, 80. *See also* Odo
Beauchamp, Hugh de, s. Beds and/or Bucks, 25, 28
    Nicholas de, 75
    Walter de, s. Worcs, 87
    William de, s. Worcs, 75, 88
Beaufou, Ralph de, s. Norf, 61; ? s. Suff, 76, 77
Beaumais, Richard de, bishop of London, s. Salop, 15,
    17, 71, 72
    Philip de, ? s. Staffs or Worcs, 75, 88
Becket, Gilbert, s. London/Midd, 58
    Thomas [later archbishop of Canterbury], 58
Bedfordshire, sheriffs of, 14, 25
Belet, John, ? s. Berks, 27
Bellême, Robert de *see* Montgomery
Berkshire, sheriffs of, 26–7
Bermondsey, Surrey, priory, 78
Bernai, Ralph de, s. Heref, 45
Bernard the scribe, 33, 74
Bernicia, ancient kingdom of, 9
Bertram, Robert, s. Northumb, 66
Bigod, Hugh, earl of Norfolk, 13; s. Norf, 62; s. Suff,
    77
    Roger, 15–16; s. Norf and Suff, 60, 61, 76, 77
    William, ? s. Norf, 61; ? s. Suff, 77
Blacuin, s. Cambs, 29
Bletchingdon, Oxon, 69
Blosseville, Jordan de, s. Lincs, 55
Blund, Robert, s. Norf, 60
Bocco, Landric de, Ralph son of, s. Sussex, rape of
    Bramber, 81
Boivill, Richer de, 31
Bosham, Sussex, 80
Boulogne, count of *see* Eustace, son of King Stephen,
    and Constance his wife
Bramber, Sussex, rape of, sheriffs of, 81
Braose, Philip de, 81
    William de, 81
Brettevilla, Gilbert de, ? s. Berks, 26
Brictric, ? s. Glos, 42
Brithstan, ? s. London/Midd, 59
Brittany, count of *see* Alan
Bromham, Wilts, manor, 85
Bruning, s. Heref, 45
Buccuinte (Bucca Lincta), Andrew, justiciar of
    London, ? s. Essex, 40
Buceus, s. Sussex, rape of Bramber, 81
Bucherell, Geoffrey, s. London/Midd, 58
Buckingham, earl of, 12
Buckinghamshire, sheriffs of, 14, 28
Buckland (Book), Hugh of, 14, 16, 17; ? canon of St
    Paul's cathedral, London, 14; ? justice,
    London, 57; ? s. Beds, 25; s. Berks, 26;
    s. Bucks, 28; s. Essex, 39, 40, 77; ? s. Herts,

47; s. London/Midd, 56, 57
    William of, 23 n. 119; s. Berks, 26; s. Bucks, 28
Bulmer, Anschetil of, steward of Robert Fossard, 17;
    s. Yorks, 90
    Bertram of, s. Yorks, 90
Burg, Serlo de, 23 n. 119; s. Derb and Notts, 34, 68
Buron, Erneis de, s. Yorks, 89
Bury St Edmunds, Suff, abbey, 76
    abbot of *see* Anselm

Cahagnes, William de, s. Northants, 63, 83
Calne, Wilts, court held at, 22 n. 111
Cambridge, Cambs, lawmen of, 29
    priory of St Radegund in, 30
    charter issued at, 29
    court held at, 22 n. 111
Cambridgeshire, sheriffs of, 14, 29–30
Camville, Richard de, s. Berks, 27
Canterbury, archbishop of, 17. *See also* Becket,
        Thomas; Dunstan, Ralph; Stigand;
        Theobald; William
Canterbury, Kent, governor (*satrapa*) of *see* Aethelnoth
    cathedral priory of Christ Church in, 10
Canwell, Staffs, priory, 75
Caperun, Wymerus, ? s. Norf, 62
Capra, William, s. Som, 73
Carlisle, Cumb, 19
    sheriffs of, 31
Catmore, Adam of, s. Berks, 27
Chalford, Oxon, 69
Charwelton, Northants, 21 n. 73
Cheshire, sheriffs of, 12, 19, 32
Chesney, family, 13 and 21 n. 54
    John de, *alias* John FitzRobert, John son of Robert
        FitzWalter, 21 n. 54; s. Norf, 61; s. Suff, 77
    William de, 21 n. 54, 70; s. Norf, 62; s. Suff, 77
Chester, bishops of *see* Robert; Roger
Chester, Ches, abbey of St Werburgh in, 32
Chester, earls of *see* Avranches, Hugh d'; Ranulf I;
        Ranulf II
Chichester, bishops of *see* [Hilary]; Ralph
Clapa, Osgod, staller, 22 n. 113
Clarus, Baldwin son of, s. Berks, 27
Cleeve, Old, Som, royal manor, 73
Clent, Worcs, 75, 87
Clifford, Heref, 45
Clifton [Campville], Staffs, royal manor, 75
Clinton, Geoffrey de, s. Warw, 83
Cnut, king of England, 9, 10, 11, 17
Colchester, Essex, 40
Cole, 85
Colne, Earls, Essex, 26, 40
Comin, William, s. Worcs, 15, 88
Corbridge, Aluric of, s. Northumb, 65

FitzTetbald, Robert, s. Sussex, rape of Arundel, 81
FitzTurold, Ilbert, 45
    Gilbert, 45
FitzWalter, Fulk, s. London/Midd, 58
    Robert, s. Norf and Suff, 21 n. 54, 61, 77
        John son of, *alias* John FitzRobert, *see* Chesney, John de
        William son of *see* Chesney, William de
FitzWymarc, Robert, staller, s. Essex, 20 n. 35, 22 n. 113, 39
        Sweyn (Suen) son of, s. Essex, 39
Flambard, Rannulf, bishop of Durham, 14, 38, 78
Fontains, Fulkwinus de, ? s. Norf, 61
Fossard, Robert, steward of *see* Bulmer, Anschetil of
Freckenham, Suff, 29
Fresney (Frehnei), William de, s. Suff, 62, 77
Frewin, s. Corn, 33
Froger, s. Berks, 26
Fulk nephew of Gilbert [the knight], 61; s. Cambs, 20 n. 49; 29; s. Hunts, 48; s. Surrey, 78
Fulk, s. Cambs, 29
Fulk, s. Hunts, 49
Fulk, s. Salop, 71, 72
Furneaux, Geoffrey de, 22 n. 92; s. Corn, 33; s. Devon, 36
Furness, Lancs, abbey, 52 n. 2

Gant, Gilbert de, 55
    Walter de, 18, 55
Garsington, Oxon, 70
Geoffrey, bishop of Durham, 38
Geoffrey l'Abbé, steward of the earl of Leicester, 21 n. 52; s. Leics, 53
Geoffrey, s. Bucks, 28
Gerard, archbishop of York, 53, 65, 89
Gervase, abbot of Westminster, 58, 80
Gilbert, earl of Pembroke, 80
Gilbert the knight, 12, 17; s. Cambs, 29; s. Hunts, 48; s. Surrey, 78
    nephew of *see* Fulk
Gilbert, s. Durham, 38
Gilbert, ? s. Heref, 45
Gilbert, ? s. Northumb, 65
Gilbert, s. Sussex, rape of Pevensey, 82
Giso, bishop [of Wells], 73
Gloucester, Glos, abbey of St Peter in, 87
    monk of *see* Hugh de Port
    castle, 16
Gloucester, earl of, 12. *See also* Robert
Gloucester, Miles son of Walter of, earl of Hereford, 18; s. Glos, 42; ? s. Heref, 46; s. Staffs, 75
    Roger son of *see* Roger, earl of Hereford
    Walter son of *see* Walter, earl of Hereford
    Walter of, s. Glos, 42

Gloucestershire, sheriffs of, 16, 17–18, 42–3
Godfrey, s. Lancs, 52
Godric, Aluric son of, s. Cambs, 29, 48
Godric *dapifer*, ? s. Norf, 60; ? s. Suff, 76
Godric, ? s. Beds, 25; ? s. Berks, 15, 26; ? s. Bucks, 28
Godricson (Godricsone), Aluric *see* Godric, Aluric son of
Godwin, s. Som, 73
Gornay, Robert de, s. Som, 73
Goscelin, s. Norf, 60
Gosfregth, ? portreeve of London, s. London/Midd, 56
Gotse, Richard son of, 34; ? s. Notts, 67
Grandmesnil, Hugh de, ? s. Leics, 53
    Ivo de, ? s. Leics, 53
Gregory, s. London/Midd, 59
Grimbald, Robert, steward of Simon of Senlis, earl of Northampton, 21 n. 52; ? s. Hunts, 49; s. Northants, 64
Grip, Hugh son of, 37, 44
    Hadewise wife of Hugh, 44
'Gualdi', William, 35
Guildford, Surrey, 16
Gulafre, Philip, 21 n. 54
    Roger, ? s. Norf, 21 n. 54, 62
Gundulf, bishop of Rochester, 28, 29
Gunter, abbot of Thorney, 21 n. 73

Hacon, William son of, s. Lincs, 55
Haia, Roger, 81
Haimo I *dapifer*, s. Kent, 50
Haimo II *dapifer*, s. Kent, 50, 51
Hampshire, sheriffs of, 44
Hanslope, Michael of, castellan of Rockingham, 63
    Walter of, 63
Happisburgh, Norf, 60
Harding, s. Derb, 34
Harold, king of England, sons of, 35
Harthacnut, king of England, 60
Hastings, Sussex, rape of, sheriffs of, 81
Hastings, Ingelran of *see* Ingelramnus
Hatch (Haeccan), Hants, 85
Haverhill, Brihtmar of, 59
Hay, Roger, ? s. Sussex, 81
Heche, s. Devon, 35
Helgot, ? s. Derb, 34; s. Notts, 67
[Hemingford], Payn [of], ? s. Cambs, 29; s. Hunts, 49; s. Surrey, 79
Henry I, king of England, 10, 12, 13, 14, 16, 17, 18, 37, 40, 45, 57, 60, 61, 69, 71, 72, 75, 78, 80, 86
    Matilda daughter of *see* Matilda, Empress
    Reginald son of *see* Reginald, earl of Cornwall
Henry II, king of England, (before accession) 15, 17, 52; (as king) 10, 12, 13, 14, 58, 71, 72
Henry, son of David I, king of Scotland, 66

Herbert, bishop [of Norwich], 77
Hereford, bishops of see Robert; Roger
Hereford, earls of see Gloucester, Miles of; Roger;
    Walter
Herefordshire, sheriffs of, 11, 45–6
Heriz, Ivo de, s. Derb and Notts, 34, 68
    Robert de, s. Notts, 67
Hertford, Ilbert de, s. Herts, 47
Hertfordshire, sheriffs of, 14, 47
[Hilary], bishop of Chichester, ? s. Sussex, 81
Hildret, 23 n. 122; s. Carlisle/Cumb, 31
    Odard son of, 31
Hoel, 81
Holborn, Wolfric of, ? s. London/Midd, 56
Holderness, Yorks, 15
Hubert, Roger nephew of, ? s. London/Midd, 57, 58
Hugh, abbot of St Benet of Hulme, 62
Hugh, bishop of Durham, 38
Hugh the priest see Leicester, Hugh of
Hugh the sheriff, 44
    Hadewisa wife of, 44
    Simon son of, 44
Hugh, s. Dorset, 37
Hugh, s. Sussex, rape of Lewes, 82
Huitdeniers, Osbert, s. London/Midd, 58
[Hulme], St Benet [of], Norf, abbot of, see Hugh
Humphrey the chamberlain, ? s. Norf and Suff, 60, 76
Humphrey, ? reeve of Droitwich, ? s. Heref, 45;
    ? s. Worcs, 87
Huntingdon, Hunts, mills at, 29
Huntingdon, earl of, 12. See also Senlis, Simon de
Huntingdon, Roger of, s. Cambs, Hunts and ? Surrey,
    29, 48
Huntingdonshire, sheriffs of, 14, 29, 48–9
Huse, Walter, ? s. Som, 73; s. Wilts, 85
    William, 73

Ilbert, ? s. Heref, 45
Ingelramnus, alias Ingelran of Hastings, s. Sussex, rape
    of Hastings, 81
Ilger, Rannulf brother of, s. Hunts, 48
Inkberrow, Worcs, 87
Islington, Midd, 60
Ivry, Roger d', 35

John, bishop of Bath [and Wells], 73
John, s. Heref, 45
John, s. London/Midd, 58
John, s. Oxon, 70
John, under-s. London, 57

Kenilworth, Warw, priory, 83
Kent, 9
    sheriffs of, 50–1

Keynsham, Som, royal manor, 73
Keyston, Hunts, royal manor, 48
Kilpeck, Hugh of, 46
Kineward, ? s. Berks, 22 n. 113
Kingsley, Staffs, 75
Kingston, Sussex, 81
Kinric, ? s. Hunts, 22 n. 113
Kinver, Ger' of, ? s. Staffs, 75

Lacy, Hugh de, ? Heref, 45
    Robert de, 18; ? s. Northumb, 65; ? s. Yorks, 89
Lancashire, sheriffs of, 19, 52
Langetot, Aliz de, 70
Laurence, abbot of Westminster, 59
Lauro, Kineward de, ?? s. Berks, 22 n. 113; s. Worcs,
    87
Leicester, earl of, 12
    stewards of see Ralph the butler: Geoffrey l'abbé
Leicester, Hugh of, alias Hugh the priest, 15; steward
    of Matilda of Senlis, 17; s. Leics, 53; s. Lincs,
    55; s. Northants, 63; s. Warw, 83
Leicestershire, sheriffs of, 53
LeLutre, William, s. London/Midd, 58
Lenton, Notts, priory, 53
Leofcild, s. Essex, 39
Leofric, s. Heref, 45
Leofric, s. Kent, 50
Leofric, s. Worcs, 87
Leofstan, reeve of London, ? s. London/Midd, 57
Leofstan, ? s. Suff, 76
Lewes, Sussex, priory, 82
Lewes, rape of, sheriffs of, 82
Limesi, Ralph de, ? s. Hants, 44
Lincoln, bishop of see Remigius; Robert
Lincoln, Merlosuein of, s. Lincs, 15, 54
    Wigod of, s. Lincs, 55
Lincolnshire, sheriffs of, 54–5
Liulf, 65
Logis, Odard de, lord of Wigton, 31
London, bishop of see Beaumais, Richard de
London, Baynard's castle, castellans of see Bainard,
    Ralph and William
    cathedral church of St Paul in, ? canon of see Osbert
        the priest
    chamberlain of see William the chamberlain
    church of St Martin le Grand in, ? canon of see
        Montacute, Richard of
    reeves of, 56. See also Leofstan
London and Middlesex, sheriffs of, 13, 56–9
Lucy (Luci), Richard de, justiciar, Essex, 13; s. Essex,
    41
Lyoth, Hugh, ? s. Essex, 40; ? s. Suff, 77

Maenfenin, s. Beds and Bucks, 25, 28

Pevensey, rape of, sheriffs of, 80, 82
Pevensey, Drogo of, s. Sussex, rape of Hastings, 81
    Simon son of, s. Sussex, rape of Hastings, 81
Peverel, William, 16, 34, 53, 67
Picot, s. Cambs, 29
Picot, Ralph, s. Kent, 51
    Robert, ? s. Northumb, 65
    Roger, ? s. Northumb, 65
Picquigny, Ansculf de, s. Bucks, 28; s. Surrey, 78
    William de, s. Surrey, 78
Piddlehinton, Dorset, 37
Pîtres, Roger de, ? s. Berks, 26; s. Glos, 42
    Walter son of, 42
Podiis, Jordan de, ? s. Berks, 27
Poitou, Roger of see Montgomery
Ponhar, Walter, 63
Pont de l'Arche, William de, s. Berks, 27; s. Hants and
    chamberlain of the treasury at Winchester,
    16, 20 n. 49, 44, ? s. Sussex, 80; s. Wilts, 85
Port, Adam de, ? s. Heref, 45
    Henry de, 44
    Hubert de, 76
    Hugh de, ? s. Devon, 35; ? s. Hants, 44, 85;
        ? s. Kent, 50; ? s. Lincs, 54; ? s. Notts, 67;
        vicarius of Winchester, later monk of
        St Peter's abbey, Gloucester, 44
Proudfoot (Prutfot, Prutfort), Gilbert, ? s. London/
    Midd, 57, 58

Raddon, Richard de, s. Corn, 33; s. Dorset, 37, 86
'Radulphus' (? Ranulf), vicomte of Avranches, 32
Raimes, Roger de, 56
Rainer, ? s. London/Midd, 57
Ralph, archbishop [of Canterbury], 40
Ralph, bishop of Chichester, 80, 81
Ralph, earl [of East Anglia], 15, 60
Ralph the butler, steward of the earl of Leicester, 53
Ralph, ? s. Berks, 26
Ralph, ? s. Cambs, 30; ? s. Surrey, 79
Ralph, ? s. Leics, 53
Ralph, ? s. Lincs, 55
Ralph, ? s. Warw, 83
Ralph, ? s. Yorks or Richmond, 90
Ramsey, Hunts, abbey, abbots of see Ailsi; Aldwin;
    Walter
Ranulf I Meschin, earl of Chester, 31, 32, 55
Ranulf II, earl of Chester, 32, 52
Ranulf, s. Ches, 32
Ranulf, s. London/Midd, 58, 79
Ranulf, s. Surrey, 16, 78
Ranulf, s. Sussex, rape of Pevensey, 82
Reading, Berks, abbey, 46
Redvers family, 16
    Baldwin de, 35
    Richard de, s. Devon, 36

Reginald, earl of Cornwall, 33
Reinbert, steward and sheriff of the count of Eu,
    s. Sussex, rape of Chichester, 81
Remigius, bishop of Lincoln, 29, 67
Restold, s. Oxon, 17, 70
Richard the chaplain, s. Glos, 42
Richard, s. Bucks, 28
Richard, s. Derb, 34
Richard, ? canon of Salisbury cathedral, ? s. Wilts, 15,
    86
Richardiville, Walter de, s. Sussex, rape of Lewes, 82
Richer, s. Carlisle/Cumb, 31
Richmond, Yorks, sheriff of see Ralph
Richmond, earl of, 90
Ridel, Geoffrey, 63
    Geva, 75
Robert, bishop of Chester, 34
Robert, bishop of Hereford, 45
Robert, bishop of Lincoln, 28, 55, 63
Robert, bishop of St Andrews, 90
[Robert], count of Mortain, 33
Robert, [earl of] Gloucester, 14
Robert, duke [of Normandy], 67
Robert the staller, 39
Robert, s. Staffs, 75
Robert, ? s. Sussex, rape of Pevensey, 82
Rochester, bishop of, 10; see also Gundulf
Rochester, Kent, monastery of St Andrew in, 10
Rockingham, Northants, castellan of see Hanslope,
    Michael of
Roger, bishop of Chester, 75
Roger, bishop of Salisbury, 14
Roger, earl of Hereford, 18; ? s. Glos, 42
    stewards of see Maurice; Westbury, Osbert of
Roger, s. Hunts, 48
    G. son of, s. Hunts, 48
Roger, ? s. London/Midd, 56, 57
Roger, ? s. Oxon, 69
Roger, s. Surrey, 78
Roger, ? s. Warw, 83
Rouen, Normandy, vicomte of see Anselm
Rualon, s. Kent, 50
Rutland, 19, 67

Sackville, William de, 40
St Albans, Herts, abbey, 25
St Andrews, Scotland, bishop of see Robert
Saint Clair, Haimo de, ? s. Essex, 40
St John, John of, 70
    Thomas of, s. Oxon, 16, 69
    William of, 81
        Roger de la Haye, brother of, 81
St Michael's Mount, Corn, priory, 33
Saint Sauveur, Normandy, lord of see Nigel the vicomte
Salisbury, bishops of see Osmund; Roger

Waverley, Surrey, abbey, 79
Wedmore, Som, church of, 73
Wells, bishop of *see* Giso, John, bishop of Bath
Westbury, Osbert of, steward of Roger earl of
        Hereford, 21 n. 52; s. Glos, 42
Westminster, Midd, abbey, 11, 16, 67
   abbot of *see* Crispin, Gilbert; Gervase; Laurence
   ecclesiastical council of (1175), 14
Westmorland, 19
Wetheral, Cumb, priory, 31
Wibert, William son of, ? s. Sussex, 80
Wigton, Cumb, lord of *see* Odard de Logis
William, archbishop of Canterbury, 12, 72
William [of St Calais], bishop of Durham, 65
William [of Ste Barbe], bishop of Durham, 38
William, bishop of Exeter, 33
W[illiam], bishop of Norwich, 62
William, count of Aumale, 90
William, count of Mortain, 33, 57, 82
William I, king of England, 11, 12, 14, 15, 16, 17, 20 n.
    35, 25, 37, 39, 44, 48, 50, 56, 65, 76, 80, 89
William II, king of England, 11, 12, 14, 16, 17, 31, 52,
    85
William, son of King Stephen, 52, 80
William the chamberlain of London, ? s. London/
    Midd, 57
William, s. Beds, 25
William, s. Durham, 38
William, s. Kent, 51
William, s. Norf, 62

William, s. Oxon, 69
William, s. Sussex, rape of Lewes, 82
William, ? s. Warw, 84
William, s. Wilts, 85
William, ? s. Yorks, 90
Wiltshire, 13
   sheriffs of, 85–6
Winchester, Hants, 81
   castle, 44
   royal treasury at, 16, 44
   vicarius of *see* Hugh de Port
Winchester, Richard of, ? s. Beds, 25, 28
Winebald, ? s. Ches, 32
Winsford, Som, royal manor, 73
Worcester, bishop of, 16, 87
Worcester, Worcs, castle, 16, 87
   cathedral church of, lands of, 17, 75, 87
Worcestershire, sheriffs of, 16, 87–8
Wouldham, Kent
Wulfgar the portreeve *see* Ulf
Wulfsige the priest, shireman/s. Kent, 9, 10, 14, 50
Wymer *capellanus*, 62
Wymond, ? s. Surrey, 78

York, abbey of St Mary in, 31
   abbot of *see* Stephen
York, archbishop of *see* Ealdred; Gerard; Thomas
Yorkshire, 9, 15
   sheriffs of, 89–90
Ypres, William of, ? s. Kent, 51

Printed in the United Kingdom for HMSO.
Dd.291116, 8/90, C6, 3390/3, 5673, 117618.